From Worrier to Warrior

A Guide to Conquering Your Fears

by
Dan Peters, Ph.D.

Great Potential Press™

From Worrier to Warrior: A Guide to Conquering Your Fears

Edited by: Jennifer Ault
Interior design: The Printed Page
Cover design: Hutchison-Frey
All illustrations by Tracy Hill, © 2013

Published by Great Potential Press, Inc.
1325 N. Wilmot Road, Suite 300
Tucson, AZ 85712
www.greatpotentialpress.com

Printed and bound in the United States of America using partially recycled paper.

17 16 15 14   5 4 3 2

At the time of this book's publication, all facts and figures cited are the most current available. All telephone numbers, addresses, and website URLs are accurate and active; all publications, organizations, websites, and other resources exist as described in this book; and all have been verified as of the time this book went to press. The author(s) and Great Potential Press make no warranty or guarantee concerning the information and materials given out by organizations or content found at websites, and we are not responsible for any changes that occur after this book's publication. If you find an error or believe that a resource listed here is not as described, please contact Great Potential Press.

Great Potential Press provides a wide range of authors for speaking events. To find out more, go to www.greatpotentialpress.com/do-you-need-a-speaker, email info@greatpotentialpress.com, or call (520) 777-6161.

Library of Congress Cataloging-in-Publication Data

Peters, Daniel B., 1970-
  From worrier to warrior : a guide to conquering your fears / Dan Peters, PhD.
pages cm
  Includes bibliographical references and index.
  Audience: Age 8-16
  Audience: Grade 7 to 8.
  ISBN 978-1-935067-24-5 (pbk.) -- ISBN 1-935067-24-9 (pbk.) 1. Worry in children—Juvenile literature. 2. Fear in children—Juvenile literature. 3. Anxiety in children—Juvenile literature. I. Title.
  BF723.W67P468 2014
  155.4'1246--dc23
2013031659

Dedication

For my children,
Sadie, Joe, and Tobie,
and for the courageous young people whose victories over monsters
I have had the privilege to witness. You all inspire me.

Table of Contents

Acknowledgments

Many people helped me to write this book—some of them without even knowing it. Several pioneers have worked to help people overcome their worry, anxiety, and fear, and much of what I have learned has come from them. In particular, I have been influenced by a course of study called Phobease™, developed by Dr. Howard Liebgold, a physician from California. Affectionately known as Dr. FEAR (False Exaggerations Appearing Real), Dr. Liebgold taught Phobease classes for more than 25 years, helping more than 19,000 adults and children to successfully conquer their fears. I have worked with individuals who have taken his classes and have heard first-hand about the positive impact he has had on their lives. Sadly, Dr. Liebgold passed away just prior to the publication of this book. It is my hope that this book continues the important work that he began and to which he dedicated his life.

My work also has been influenced by Jackie Persons, co-founder and Director of the Center for Cognitive Therapy in San Francisco, who taught me that I had to establish a trusting relationship with my clients for cognitive behavioral strategies to work effectively, as well as Jeff Zimmerman, Vickie Dickerson, and John Neal, of the Mental Research Institute (MRI) in Palo Alto, who taught me that instead of focusing on what is "wrong" with people,

people can be empowered to make changes using their strengths and focusing on what is "right" with them.

This book came out of a collaboration in Napa to break the silence on anxiety and other mental health issues and to get more children and teens support. Spearheading the grassroots-led community change work projects is the Director of Somos Napa/We Are Napa, Debbie Alter-Starr, MSW, LCSW. She first led a project to make a DVD titled *Taming the Worry Monster*, which was used by the Napa Valley Unified School District, Napa County Office of Education, and Napa Valley TV in both Spanish and English. Debbie also started programs to teach children and teens the techniques in this book, and she continues to advocate for more prevention programs. The goal is to encourage interested parents and teens to help change how communities address emotional health issues. Websites for ideas of how to do this are listed in the back of this book.

Many thanks to the collaborative partners: Napa Valley Unified School District, Napa County Office of Education, and Napa Valley TV. Special thanks to James Raymond, Executive Director of Napa Valley TV and Napa Valley Media, and his staff for their expertise and for transcribing the DVD, which became the foundation for this book. I am particularly indebted to Debbie for introducing me to Dr. Liebgold's work and for her continued creative ideas that have fueled my passion for helping people overcome anxiety and maximize their developmental potential, as well as contributing to fostering healthy communities.

I am grateful to the amazing group of people at Great Potential Press. First, to my publishers, Jim Webb and Jan Gore, for believing in the importance of this book and for their ideas, skill, and collaborative approach. They have put together an amazing team of individuals. I am grateful to all of them, and here I will highlight a few. I need to acknowledge Jen Ault, by far the most passionate editor in the world. Jen's commitment to this project was contagious, and it was a very meaningful collaboration. Thank you to Julee Hutchison for helping to bring the Worry Monster to life and for her patience and guidance in the process. Thank you to Katrina Durham for her ideas, support, and for helping to spread the word. And finally, thank you to Lisa Liddy for her diligence in laying out the book and for putting everything in just the right place.

I am grateful to my friends and colleagues who reviewed the original manuscript and offered wonderful suggestions: Debbie Alter-Starr, Joanna Haase, Dana Cope, Laura Masters, and Kim Demus, and to my junior reviewers Jack Roy Cope, Lily Demus, and Ella and JJ Cline. This book is made real by the authentic stories of special and courageous kids and their parents, whose stories are highlighted within its pages. You know who you are. You are an inspiration to me and now will be an inspiration to many who are trying to drive the Worry Monster away.

A special thank-you goes to my colleague Sally Baird for her support and collaboration in helping children and families take on and fight the Worry Monster. I would also like to thank three mentors, Anita Green, Allen Ewig, and Steve Hobbs, as well as my friends and colleagues Ed Amend and Susan Daniels, who have offered encouragement and support at crucial points in my life. I am also grateful for the dedicated friendship and support of Scott Tredennick, Rich Weingart, and my brother Mitch Peters.

Finally, this book would not be possible without the support of my family: to my kids, Sadie, Joe, and Tobie, for teaching me about the Worry Monster, how to help them (and how not to help them), and for their permission to tell their stories. Thank you to my parents, Mady and Richard, for their unwavering and unconditional love, interest, and support in my career and life. Last, but far from least, I thank my wife Lizzie, without whom all would not be possible. She is my partner in life, my business partner, my editor, and my friend who is committed to raising healthy kids and helping others do the same.

Introduction

Worry is like a rocking chair. It will give you something to do, but it won't get you anywhere.

~ Proverb

Hi there! My name is Dan. Some people call me Dr. Dan, others call me Coach Dan, and others just call me Dan. I am a psychologist, which means that I help people understand themselves better, learn how their mind works, and find ways to achieve their goals in life. I basically act as a coach by helping people learn strategies to worry less and enjoy life more. If you are reading this book right now, it probably means that someone who cares about you wants you to be able to enjoy life with fewer worries and fears. Or it may mean that you yourself have made the courageous decision to take steps to reduce the amount of worry and fear in your life. In either case, I want you to know that there is hope for you to accomplish this goal. That's the reason I wrote this book—to help children, adolescents, and young adults overcome worry and fear.

So How Did I Become an Anxiety Expert?

Even though I am now an adult who helps people overcome worry and fear, I experienced a lot of anxiety (a fancy name for worry and fear) as a child. I didn't know what it was called when I was young, but I knew that there was something strange that was often with me—something that made me feel a certain way, caused me to think certain thoughts, and made me do (or not do) certain things. Early in my life, I remember how important it was to me to follow the rules and do the "right" things. I was always very aware of my surroundings, what others were doing (or not doing), and what was "supposed" to happen. I remember being sent out of my second-grade classroom for talking just *once*! I was devastated and sat in the hallway crying. It was the end of the world, right? It sure felt like it then.

In school, I always hated to read and write. (And of course, a lot of what you do in school is reading and writing.) Writing was hard for me, and I could never get my thoughts down on paper. I would sit staring at the blank page as my chest tightened and time ticked away. Reading also took a lot of energy. I would skim what I could, but I mostly tried to avoid the longer reading assignments. I felt nervous that my teacher would discover that I wasn't doing the reading. I don't know how many excuses I had to come up with to tell my parents why I wasn't reading.

Another problem was tests. Tests were nerve-wracking because I was always worried that I wouldn't have enough time to finish— which was true; I almost never finished on time. It turns out that I'm dyslexic (I read very slowly) and dysgraphic (it's hard for me to write what I am thinking). I experienced first-hand the worry and anxiety that comes with learning challenges and the fear of not doing well and then being found out. I worried a lot every day!

Other people, however, did not know how much I worried. I remember one of my cousins saying to me, "What's it like to always do everything right?" I wasn't sure what she meant. Was there any other way? Was I really doing everything right? Was I thought of as perfect by everybody? I didn't realize at the time how hard I worked and how much effort it took to make sure I did everything "right." I was an expert at thinking of all of the possibilities of what I should say and do so everything would be fine.

I have a vivid memory of lying in bed at night while in seventh grade. I distinctly remember going over my list of things to worry about. When I got to the end of the list, I realized that I had checked all of them off—I had worried about each thing on the list, and so I was done worrying. I felt a wonderful sense of calm. But then, as quick as that feeling of peace came, it was gone because my next thought was, "So what *else* do I need to worry about so that everything will be okay?" As you may already know, worrying is a full time job! Back then, I didn't know that there was any other way to think and feel.

I played competitive tennis as a teen. My coaches often wondered why I was not able to consistently perform in match play like I did in practice. They didn't realize (and neither did I) that I was so often worrying about losing that I wasn't able to focus on playing the game. I practiced a lot and had natural abilities, yet fear and worry (also known as the Worry Monster) often kept me from maximizing my potential. I played fearlessly in practice, because in practice, I had nothing to lose. Fear of failure didn't apply in practice, but it sure did during tournaments. I thought, *What if I let my coach down? What will my parents think since they spent so much time, energy, and money supporting me for nothing?*

Years later I was in graduate school learning how to be a psychologist. Graduate school is where you go after college if you want to get a higher degree. I sat in my classes frustrated with my lack of knowledge. I read everything I could on every subject I studied, because we all know that in order to do well in a class, you need to know *everything* about the subject, right? Wrong! It wasn't until much later, when I learned that I was a perfectionist, that I realized I had been comparing myself to my professors and supervisors who had been in the field 15-30 years. I'd felt that I had to know what they knew, even though I was in my early twenties and only in graduate school. As you can see, the Worry Monster and I go way back. He was a regular visitor of mine for years and years and years.

Have you had any of the experiences or feelings that I've had? I am guessing that some of them may be the same. Many could be different, too, but all of us worriers share common traits—we feel nervous, worry about bad things happening, avoid certain activities, and spend a lot of energy hoping things will turn out "right" or "perfect." And there is something else that we all have in common: we are smart, conscientious, honest, and hardworking people. It's true! People who worry tend to have those characteristics. What really bothers me, though, is that the Worry Monster, who you are going to learn about, picks on good people like us. That's one of the reasons I am passionate about helping people like you get rid of him and get him out of your life—for good!

It's not easy growing up. As we get older, there is a strong need to fit in and be accepted by our peers. Adolescence can be a particularly challenging time, since we are trying to figure out who we are, who and what we like, and who our real friends are. While those things can be hard at many periods of life, middle school can be especially rough. Kids that age tend to focus on pointing out differences in others, and they like to travel in groups so they feel better about themselves. It's hard to not have a group to be with, and it can be equally hard to stay in a group once you find one. Common worries during these difficult years are worrying about how you look, whether or not you are going to be accepted, whether you will be invited to parties, and being teased or bullied. Although they are common, worries about all of these things can be stressful and painful and can take up a lot of your mental energy. Another important thing to know is that if we are anxious and stressed for a long period of time, we can become depressed. Our brains and bodies can only run in high gear for so long before burning out. These are all important reasons to learn strategies to fight and conquer the Worry Monster.

I am still a pretty good worrier, but I work hard to keep the Worry Monster away by using the tools that I am going to teach you in this book. Since worry seems to run in families, my children, ages nine, 11, and 13, have plenty of experience with the Worry Monster, too. You will read about some of their experiences in this book. They were afraid of things like new situations, being left at school, trying new activities, speaking or performing in front of others, answering the phone, looking directly at people, making a mistake, getting in trouble, and the list goes on. Do any of these sound familiar? No matter what your worry or fears, you are going to learn strategies to make them go away. There is only one thing you will need, and that is courage. The Worry Monster is a bully who likes people to be scared of him, and just like a bully, he backs off when we show him that we are brave enough to stand up to him.

Why This Book?

You are not alone in your worries. Lots of other kids have worries like you do. Eight out of every 100 teenagers have been diagnosed with anxiety, and their symptoms (worry and scared feelings) usually start by the time they are six years old. Also, 18 out of 100 adults are diagnosed with anxiety every year—that's about 40 million people![1] And these percentages only count the people who go to doctors for their symptoms, not all of the others who suffer quietly and alone and don't get help. That means there are literally millions upon millions of people in this world who feel like you do. There is nothing to be ashamed of since so many others can relate to your worried and scared feelings. You also will find that the more people you share your worries and fears with, the more that others will share their worries and fears with you.

In spite of the fact that millions of young people and adults worry and feel scared, I haven't found anything positive about worrying and being scared yet. Worrying keeps us from being who we really are and from who we can be. Worrying literally drains our energy and makes us afraid to take the risks we need to take to grow. Worry and fear keep us down, scared, miserable, and insecure with ourselves and our abilities. The good news is that you can change all of this.

I have had the privilege of working with hundreds of courageous young people like you each year to help them battle and defeat the Worry Monster. How do I do it? By helping them change from worriers to warriors. I teach them how to defeat the Worry Monster. Through my own experiences with worry and anxiety, watching what it does to my children, and seeing how it affects the many children and families I have worked with over the years, I have become committed to helping people get rid of worry and anxiety for good. I believe that the strategies you will learn in this book will help you to do this.

About This Book

This book is a "How To" book designed to help you over-come worry and fear by teaching you a number of easy-to-follow strategies. I've seen many kids drive the Worry Monster away with these techniques. You can read the book and learn the strategies by yourself, or you can read it with your parents or another trusted adult. You will learn about how our bodies are programmed to keep us alive and that we go into "survival mode" (No, I am not talking about Minecraft!), even when we don't need to. You will learn about how your body feels during the "fight or flight" response and which "whoosh" feelings you experience. You will learn who the Worry Monster is and how he puts thoughts in your head that make you feel worried and scared. You will then learn how to change those worry thoughts and practice specific behaviors to make the Worry Monster go away. You will learn how to create your very own tool-box of strategies or weapons that you can carry with you so you are ready to fight the Worry Monster whenever he tries to mess with you. Further, by learning these skills, you will also be learning skills that will help you be resilient in life. This means you will know how to face and overcome whatever challenges come your way.

You can use the strategies in this book even if you are already talking to a counselor or a therapist. In fact, it might be helpful to talk to your counselor about the things you read here. That way you and your counselor can talk about as many ways to battle the Worry Monster as possible.

I have been privileged to watch many children like you defeat the Worry Monster time and time again by using the simple prin-ciples and strategies described in this book. Now it is your turn. Are you ready? Your warrior training is about to begin. It's time to take the Worry Monster down. Let's do this!

Note: If you would like to have a picture of the Worry Monster to look at and refer to as you read this book, a full-color image of him is available at http://bit.ly/KidWarrior or http://bit.ly/TheWorryMonster. You can go to either of those websites to find a pdf file, which you can print and use any time you feel that actually seeing the monster will help you do battle against him and conquer him.

CHAPTER 1

Who Is the Worry Monster?

Worry is a useless mulling over of things we cannot change.

~ Peace Pilgrim

Some Examples of Worriers

Before we learn about who the Worry Monster is, I want to tell you about a few young people I know and the different challenges they face every day.

Sierra is six years old and in first grade. She is afraid to be alone, so she follows her mother around the house and needs her to come with her into to her bedroom, and even into the bathroom. She calls to her mother when she wakes up—at all hours of the night—to come be with her. Drop-off at school is difficult because Sierra clings to her mother and says she doesn't want her to go. Sierra's mom has to stay with her at birthday parties and after-school activities or else Sierra will refuse to participate in them.

Ben is nine years old and a fourth grader. He worries about bad things happening, though he is not sure exactly what the bad things are. He is always asking his mother and his teacher for reassurance that things will be okay—

for example, that he is doing his schoolwork the way he is supposed to. Ben worries that he will get in trouble at school, and that his classmates may, too. He bites his fingernails and chews on his shirt but isn't aware he is doing so. He often complains of having a stomachache.

Tanner is 10, and he needs to be in charge of everything. Others see him as controlling and bossy but are initially drawn to him because of his energy and great ideas. Tanner has trouble keeping friends because he doesn't listen to anyone else's ideas and makes up rules to favor himself in the games he plays with others. When things don't go his way, or he loses, or kids refuse to play with him, he lashes out at them verbally and erupts emotionally. He always comes up with some reason why the other children deserved what happened or why it is their fault.

Phil is 10 and in fifth grade. He always seems to be worrying about something that could happen. He works hard to do well in school and wants to please his parents and teachers. Most people don't know how much he worries because he keeps it to himself. He frequently believes that he will stop worrying once he completes a project or after playing well in an important soccer game, but there always seems to be something new to worry about.

Jenny is 11 years old and in the sixth grade. She has started at a new middle school, and her best friends are all attending a different school. Jenny says that she feels nauseous at school and fears that she may get sick and throw up. Her teachers say she seems to be in a daze during class. Jenny often begs to stay home from school because she feels sick. When she does stay home, she seems fine. She also seems to be normal or "herself" on weekends.

Casey is 12, and she feels like she has to touch things a certain way to feel okay. If she touches one of her legs, she feels like *she has to touch the other leg in the same way so that they are balanced. When she walks into her room, she has to touch her door five times or else she feels funny. She counts numbers in her head while she's walking to school, and if she loses track of the numbers, she has to go back to the last place she remembered them and start again. She says that if she doesn't do these things, something bad might happen.*

Mateo is 15 years old, in the ninth grade, and has always struggled with social situations. He has trouble looking people in the eyes when he talks to them, and he fears that he will have nothing interesting to say or will say something stupid and be laughed at. Mateo feels like everyone else does things better than he does and that he will never achieve his goals in life. When things don't go as he plans, he becomes very upset and overwhelmed and says things like, "What if I can't take care of myself when I grow up?" and "What if I never have a meaningful friendship?" His parents say he seems to carry the weight of the world on his shoulders. He stays home after school and on weekends playing video games and cannot be encouraged to call kids he knows from school to make plans with them. He doesn't want to join activities at his school because he's sure he will be no good at them and that his classmates won't like him.

Sophie, age 17 and a junior in high school, has always been a high achiever, mostly receiving A's and A+'s in school. She also plays several sports and volunteers in the community. She is so busy and takes such hard classes that she stays up late studying because feels that she needs to do her work perfectly. Even though her work is excellent, she is rarely proud of her accomplishments. She experiences life as "a grind." She is often tense and stressed, and she worries about what will happen if she doesn't get into a top college.

The children and teenagers described here experience common worries and fears. Do any of these young people worry about the same things you do? Some children worry about their own and their loved ones' safety, others worry about making mistakes, some worry about being laughed at, and others worry about not living up to their own and others' standards. And some kids just seem to worry about everything!

Even though you may be used to worrying and being scared, I know you don't want to feel that way. It's no fun to feel nervous and scared and to have stomachaches and headaches. You are now going to take the first step in making those feeling go away. How? You are going to learn about the Worry Monster—an imaginary beast who puts thoughts in your head that make you worry and feel scared.

Here he is. Take a good look at how goofy and ridiculous he looks. He's the guy who tells you to think certain thoughts that make you feel bad and scared. I have learned through my own life, my children's lives, and the lives of hundreds of others whom I have worked with that if we realize it's the Worry Monster who is bullying us, and we learn how he works, we can make him small and powerless—and we can even make him go away completely. It takes courage and practice, but I know it works! (You can download a full-color image of the Worry Monster by visiting http://bit.ly/KidWarrior or http://bit.ly/TheWorryMonster.)

Pulling Back the Curtain

Here's an example of what I'm talking about. Have you seen the movie *The Wizard of Oz*? Remember the scene in which Dorothy, Tin Man, Scarecrow, and the Cowardly Lion are all in front of the big, bad, scary Wizard, who's making terrifying noises with smoke billowing all around him? The Wizard is being mean and not granting their wishes. They are badly frightened and shaking. The Lion doesn't have courage, the Tin Man doesn't have a heart, the Scarecrow doesn't have a brain, and Dorothy thinks she is never going to get home to see Auntie Em. Then something happens: the smallest character, Dorothy's little dog, tugs on the curtain covering the most powerful being. When Toto pulls the curtain back, they see that the Wizard is just a man working levers and controlling what they see and hear. When we see the main characters again, what do we see? All of a sudden they're not afraid anymore! They are strong, courageous, and smart! They start problem solving, and before we know it, Dorothy is on her way back home.

So there you have it. When we see how Toto helped Dorothy and her friends discover the truth, we see an example of how the Worry Monster is actually nothing to be afraid of (just like the Wizard). Now you are going to learn to uncover the monster's cowardly tricks and fight him until you take his power away. The Worry Monster is a big bully who tricks us into thinking he is powerful, when in fact we have courage in ourselves to fight him—and to cope, persevere, and

figure things out. A wise young man I know who knows the Worry Monster well told me, "We are all stronger than we think."

You can read this book alone or with one of your parents or family members, or your parents may want to read the parent version of this book. It helps to have a team to fight the Worry Monster, and the more you and your parents and family talk about him, the smaller he gets, until "poof," he finally disappears.

It is time now for us to start laughing at the Worry Monster. Let's taunt him, tease him, and tell him to stop bothering you. Worry Monster, your days are numbered!

Things to Remember

✔ The Worry Monster is a bully.

✔ The Worry Monster tricks us into feeling scared and worried.

✔ You will learn to drive the Worry Monster away and be less worried and scared.

CHAPTER 2

Anxiety and the Fear Response

Our fatigue is often caused not by work, but by worry, frustration, and resentment.

~ Dale Carnegie

Now that you know who the Worry Monster is, I want to tell you about anxiety and how it works. There are lots of definitions of anxiety, but we going to use one that is simple and makes sense in order to meet our goal—to take the Worry Monster down!

Simply put, anxiety is an irrational fear.[2] *Irrational* is another word for unreasonable—and probably not true. "They're all going to laugh at me." "Something bad is going to happen." "I'll get lost." "What if you don't come back for me?" "What if I make a mistake?" These are all examples of anxiety and fears that feel very real.

However, you are going to learn that it's the Worry Monster who tricks us into feeling these uncomfortable and scary feelings by messing with our thoughts. As you well know, some bad things seem like they really *could* happen, so the Worry Monster makes us think that those things are definitely what *will* happen. The Worry Monster's main strategy is to convince you that the *very, very, very small chance* that something bad might happen is what's *actually* going to happen and that when it does happen, the results will be awful. I know what you may be thinking: "Well, something bad *could* happen to my mom," or "My classmates *might* make fun of me," or "We *could* get in a car accident." Yes, these are all very small possibilities, but the Worry Monster tricks you into thinking that these possibilities are guaranteed to happen, and when they do happen, they will totally ruin your life. But the Worry Monster is nothing more than a bully. He bullies us into thinking certain things, feeling certain things, and then behaving in certain ways, which makes our lives harder and keeps us from experiencing joy and happiness.

The Survival Response

Now that you know what anxiety is—an irrational thought—we need to talk about an important part of our human, biological makeup: the fear response. The good thing about fear is that it keeps us alive. A long time ago, we humans were cave people and hunters and gathers. We lived among other tribes who wanted our stuff, as well as big animals who wanted to eat us. We needed (and continue to need) fear to help us survive.[3] That's why, like all other animals, we have a "fight or flight" response. We can either fight our predator or run away as fast as we can—and both responses keep us alive.

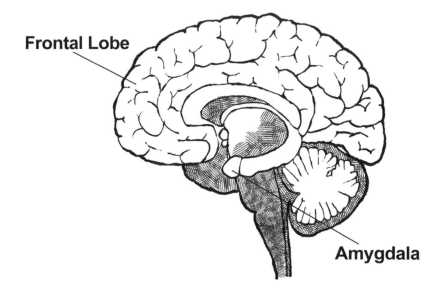

Frontal Lobe

Amygdala

Here is how our survival response works. In our brains, there is a very small almond-shaped group of neurons, called the amygdala (pronounced *uh MIG duh luh*), that resides in our limbic system, which is the emotional center of our bodies. The amygdala is the fear center of the brain. Its primary job is to sense danger and keep us alive. Imagine having a danger sensor in your head that is always turned on and always looking out for danger. That's what your amygdala does.

Here's the catch, however: when we feel fear or anxiety, we are usually *not* in a life-threatening situation, yet our amygdala is going off and the alarm bells are ringing. Let me say this very important point another way. When it comes to the Worry Monster, our amygdala is turned on and activated for action even though we don't need it to be activated. It's like having a car alarm that is too sensitive and goes off all the time over nothing. If you are walking down a dark alley and see shadows and there's no one around and you didn't bring your cell phone, that's a good time for your amygdala's alarm bells to go off. It is not practical, however, to have that same feeling when walking through the lunchroom at school with your friends. But it *feels* the same. Fortunately, most of the time we're not in dark alleys in the middle of the night.

> Amygdala *is our family's new favorite word. We all realize that it gets activated in different situations for each of us, which has been a cool discovery. We all have fears and anxiety but about different things, and now we know what is happening in our brains and not to let it control our decision to move forward. We say to each other, "My amygdala is kicking in," when something is freaking us out, and just realizing that makes it better.*
>
> ~ mother of a warrior

When the amygdala senses danger, it sends messages to our adrenal glands to start producing as much adrenaline as possible in order to help us either fight or take flight—in short, to escape quickly! It's actually quite simple, and we certainly should appreciate how our body is designed to keep us alive. When the adrenal gland gets the signal from our amygdala to pump as much adrenaline as possible, boy does it go to town, sometimes like firemen swinging a fire hose! Surges of adrenalin running through our body increase our heart rate and breathing rate and move blood from our stomach and brain into our muscles to make us stronger. We are instantly turned into running and fighting machines with one purpose: survival!

The survival response makes our body feel a certain way—and it is not very comfortable, to say the least! Here is why our body feels the way it does when we are scared:[4]

✔ *Heart and Lungs*: Your heart beats faster; your chest gets tight; you breathe faster and feel like you can't get enough air. This occurs so that you can fight and run better. Your body speeds up your heart and lungs in order to send more blood into your muscles so they are stronger.

✔ *Stomach*: You experience stomach pain, nausea, and maybe even diarrhea. This happens because much of the blood leaves your stomach and intestines and pumps into your heart, lungs, and muscles in case it is needed to turn you into a fighting and running machine. Your amygdala is more concerned with your ability to escape saber-tooth tigers than with whether you digest your macaroni and cheese.

✔ *Brain*: You feel dizzy, light-headed, and have strange feelings, like you're about to faint, you're going crazy, or you're losing control. The reason is that your blood has to leave your brain to get into your heart, lungs, and muscles.

✔ *Arms and Legs*: You start sweating and get cold hands, numbness, shaking, trembling, muscle tenseness, and even pain. The reason this happens is that your blood leaves your skin so that you won't bleed as much if you get hurt. Isn't that cool? We are so designed for survival that the blood even leaves our skin so we can do better in battle!

So as you can see, our entire body is focused on keeping us alive by diverting blood into our arms and legs so we can fight and run. Blood leaves our stomach because we don't need to digest our macaroni and cheese when we are running for our life. It makes a little more sense now, doesn't it, why you might have stomach cramps, or an upset stomach, or have to go to the bathroom over and over again. These are all symptoms that you may feel at some time or another when you're feeling worried or scared.

Next, blood leaves our brain because we don't need to solve complex problems when we are running for our lives. "No distractions! Run fast! Push hard! Harder! Faster!" But what happens? We start to feel dizzy; we start to get headaches; we start to feel like we're going nuts. Our minds are swirling because all of the blood is leaving our brains so we can run and fight—it's that simple!

Each of us has our own body reaction to anxiety. Some people's heads get hot; some have shortness of breath; others start to sweat. A 10-year-old client of mine recently described her feeling as the "whoosh" feeling because she felt like she was on a roller coaster (one she didn't want to be on!). Think about your own "whoosh" feelings. Where does the Worry Monster make you feel it in your body? How do you know when the Worry Monster is sneaking into your life and visiting you? Does your head get hot or hurt? Does your stomach feel funny or tight? Do your hands shake? Does the Worry Monster make you want to hide or run away? These are all "whoosh" feelings. Everyone feels their worry a little differently in their body. Knowing how the Worry Monster makes you feel is the first step in preparing to fight him. We are on to you, Worry Monster. You are not going to be able to be sneaky and trick us anymore!

An important thing to remember is that the scary "whoosh" feelings *always* go away. They often feel like they won't, but they do, just like an itch. One way to get through these intense and uncomfortable feelings is to "ride the wave."[5] This means just hanging on for the ride and waiting, knowing that it won't last long and will be over soon. It feels like the bad feelings will never go away, but they always do.

The Worry Monster is "turning on" your emotional brain and "turning off" your great and marvelous thinking brain. He doesn't like us to talk about him and challenge him. He doesn't like our thinking brain, and he doesn't like that we are talking about him right now. You are going to learn how to use your thinking brain to outsmart the Worry Monster so you can chase him out of town!

Things to Remember

- ✔ Our bodies are built to survive.

- ✔ The amygdala's job is to sense danger and trigger our survival or "fight or flight" response.

- ✔ Large amounts of adrenaline are activated to make us into super-human fighting or running machines.

- ✔ This adrenaline makes our body—brain, stomach, heart, lungs, arms, and legs—feel a certain way.

- ✔ We all get some type of "whoosh" feelings that let us know when the Worry Monster is visiting.

- ✔ We need to turn on our thinking brain in order to turn down our emotional brain.

- ✔ The more we talk about the Worry Monster, the weaker he gets.

CHAPTER 3

Types of Anxiety and What They Look Like

Worry does not empty tomorrow of its sorrow. It empties today of its strength.

~ Corrie Ten Boom

I have found it helpful to teach people about what the different types of worries and fears (also called anxieties) look and feel like. This is because the more we understand how the Worry Monster works on us and what strategies he uses, the stronger we get, and the less powerful he becomes. For example, I have learned that the Worry Monster sometimes makes me worry about things not working out as well as I think they should. He makes me think that I am not doing things good enough, even when I am. I also have learned that my clue is that he wakes me up in the middle of the night when it is quiet to make me worry about things, and he makes my heart beat fast when I need to be sleeping! Now that I know this about him, I have some strategies that I use to make him go away so I can get the sleep I need. We will talk about those strategies soon. But first, let's learn about the different types of anxiety people can have.

Generalized Anxiety

Generalized anxiety is basically just another way of talking about the Worry Monster. It describes what happens when a person experiences ongoing worry that is excessive and constant about most topics ("When will you be home?" "What if something bad happens?" "Do I look okay?" "What if I make a mistake?" "What if I don't get picked?"). The people with generalized anxiety are basically excellent worriers! They worry about almost everything.

> *Marcus always seems to be worrying about something. He worries that people are talking about him behind his back. He worries that he will do poorly on tests. He worries that his parents will be unhappy with his grades and that he won't ever amount to anything.*

Panic Attacks

A panic attack is when you have intense physical feelings caused by adrenalin flooding your body. A panic attack is so scary that it makes you think you might be having a heart attack, or that you might pass out, or that you might actually die. It's very scary. Panic attacks are the purest form of the fear response I told you about earlier, and they're responsible for an enormous number of visits to the emergency room—by both adults and children. There is also a less intense version of the panic attack that I refer to as an "anxiety attack." Though it's not as bad as a full-blown panic attack, it still feels awful! A lot of kids have these lower-grade versions of panic attacks when they're in anxiety-provoking situations.

> *Whenever my daughter Adrienne takes a math test, she feels dizzy; she says she can't remember what she learned and knows how to do, and she starts to think she's going to fail the test. Once she starts thinking this, she starts to sweat. Next she has trouble breathing. She tells us that she just wants to run out of the classroom, but we've encouraged her to tell her teacher that she feels sick so that she's allowed*

to go to the nurse's office instead. Her teacher is supportive and has informed us that Adrienne looks pale when this happens.

~ mother of a warrior

When I have a panic/anxiety attack, I start hyperventilating and thinking that there are going to be a whole bunch of natural disasters like tsunamis, earthquakes, fires, hurricanes, tornados, et cetera, or that there is going to be a murder or something—anything. Everything bad is going to happen.

~ 15-year-old warrior

Agoraphobia

Agoraphobia refers to when a person has a fear that he's going to have a panic attack, whether he's ever had one or not, and that he will be unable to escape the situation when he starts to panic. Because the person wants to avoid the panic attack, as well as related feelings of embarrassment, he avoids the place or situation where he fears he might experience an attack.

Agoraphobia prevents a person from going out to enjoy different activities. Let's say, for example, that someone has a panic attack in a large supermarket and then becomes afraid it is going to happen again. As a result, he refuses to go to any and all supermarkets. Next, he gets the same bodily sensations and fears when his family is in a restaurant, which has food smells similar to a supermarket, so he decides he is not going to any more restaurants. He then starts to fear a variety of other buildings. Before long, the person is approaching a full-blown agoraphobia situation like you see on TV sometimes, in which a person doesn't leave his house for several years. This is one of the main reasons why it is so important to face fears while you're young: so that they don't grow.

Autumn doesn't like going shopping at the mall anymore. She worries that she might have a panic attack and won't be able to escape. She also has started avoiding department stores and even the supermarket lately because she finds herself thinking, "It could happen there, too."

Obsessive-Compulsive Disorder (OCD)

OCD is when people have repetitive thoughts or ideas that are scary, embarrassing, and won't go away. A compulsion is a repetitive behavior that people do to relieve the anxiety or worry produced by the scary or embarrassing thought. Most people think of OCD in terms of flipping light switches on and off repeatedly or washing one's hands excessively. These are common OCD behaviors. But behind these behaviors are repetitive irrational thoughts that are very distressing and that won't go away. In most cases, the person has to do something to feel okay, like touch the doorway in a certain place when walking through it, tap each one of her legs the same number of times, or kiss both sides of her mom's or dad's face before bedtime.

> *Our son Walt is an exceptional student, athlete, and kind young man. He worries about his school performance and has to do certain things to make sure he doesn't fail or become "bad." These behaviors consist of touching everything an even number of times with both hands, repeating the last words of sentences in his head, and making sure he doesn't step over a line without repeating what he was thinking as he steps over the line. He also often has to erase words that he writes if he writes them while worrying about turning into a bad student, and he has to repeat certain things in his head a certain number of times so he feels okay.*
>
> ~ mother of a warrior

Specific Phobia

Phobia is another word for fear. A specific phobia is a fear that is extreme and unreasonable and is brought on by a specific object, like snakes or elevators, or a specific situation, like public speaking. These phobias are usually the easiest to avoid, such as avoiding insects by never going camping or avoiding planes by never flying. Some phobias are more difficult to avoid, like being afraid of dogs or loud noises, and can cause significant difficulty for you and your family.

> *My daughter's phobias have been extremely varied. She had a phobia of the number 3 when she was a preschooler—we didn't realize at the time it was a phobia, though. Later she had phobias of bugs, then snails. During the rainy season—and this was when she was eight years old—we had to pick her up and carry her from the car into buildings due to her fear of snails. Later she developed a phobia of her school principal, and it was hard to get her back to school in the fall.*
>
> ~ father of a warrior

Social Phobia

A social phobia is a persistent fear of social or performance situations in which a person is around unfamiliar people and worries about being criticized and humiliated. This is basically the fear of embarrassment or humiliation. "The kids are going to laugh at me." "They're making fun of me." "Look how they're looking at me." "I don't belong here." "What are they going to say?" "What if I look funny?" Now, there could be some truth to these statements, right? We all get these feelings from time to time, but what we're talking about when we refer to social anxiety is whether the response is extreme and interferes with a person's life or affects the person's life in a significant way. Examples of extreme social phobia behavior include refusal to go to school, refusal to participate in school activities, and refusal to go social events like birthday parties and extended family gatherings.

> *I worry about not being very good at something and then being embarrassed and having people laugh at me and make fun of me. I also worry about not being able to find*

where it is I am supposed to go or ending up in the wrong place and/or being told that I am in the wrong place in front of people (for example, going into the wrong classroom and sitting down and the teacher calls you out in front of everyone).

~ 15-year-old warrior

Post-Traumatic Stress Disorder (PTSD)

Post-Traumatic Stress Disorder, known as PTSD, is a common problem for our soldiers who have returned from war and have experienced trauma from seriously scary situations like being in a gunfight or from experiencing injuries from bombs or gunfire. But PTSD can also apply to anyone who experiences other kinds of trauma—either a near-death experience, or someone else's near-death experience, or any situation where there is intense fear. This could include being in a tornado or a car accident or even witnessing a bad accident. A person could also have PTSD after seeing a serious fight or being in a home where the family members have terrible fights. A person with PTSD may feel emotionally numb, experience nightmares, or have flashbacks of the bad experience. The person usually tries to avoid situations that remind him of the earlier traumatic event; he may be jumpy and nervous, or he may have extreme emotional meltdowns.

Ami cries uncontrollably at times, but at other times she just seems to go blank. She gets tense when she has to get in a car and sometimes refuses. She says she can't stop thinking about the car accident she and her mom were in last year and how her mother was taken away in an ambulance.

Separation Anxiety

Separation anxiety is when a child is afraid to leave her parents and feels that something bad is going to happen to her or her parents while the two of them are apart. Kids who have separation anxiety may feel that they really *need* to sleep in their parents' bed, *need* their parents to stay at school and at activities with them, and feel afraid whenever they are away from their parents.

> *Cody gets anxious at bedtime. My husband and I work late, and we have a babysitter for him—an older woman he really likes. But even with her there, Cody forces himself to stay awake until his father and I both get home and get to bed, even if it is really late, because he worries that something bad will happen to us; he can only relax once we have returned safely.*
>
> ~ mother of a warrior

Perfectionism

Perfectionism is another common way that the Worry Monster plays havoc with our lives. The main element of perfectionism is a fear of failure.[6] Some experts think that there is a good kind of perfectionism and bad kind of perfectionism.[7] Good or healthy perfectionism is when we try to be our best, like paying attention to details and working hard to make the best project we can, but not stressing out too much if it's not truly perfect. Bad or unhealthy perfectionism is the kind that makes us feel like we can never be good enough.

Other experts think that there's no such thing as good perfectionism. Let's face it: perfectionism usually makes us feel bad.[8] The goal for perfectionists should be to strive for excellence rather than for perfection because striving for excellence involves a lot of failure and risk taking.[9] In order to do anything well—play the violin, write in cursive, ride a bike, play tennis or chess—we have to practice. When we practice and when we are still learning, we make mistakes. We learn from mistakes, so there's no way anyone can be perfect at things until they've done them many times—perfection is hard to achieve. We have to take some risks to try, and then try again. People with perfectionism often are afraid to try new things because they don't want to make mistakes. They don't want to do it unless they can do it perfectly. In that way, perfectionism keeps us from perfectly. In that way, perfectionism keeps us from learning new things and having new experiences. Perfectionists have to learn that sometimes their best effort is good enough.

Lots of perfectionists accomplish one goal only to see that there is another goal they need to achieve to feel successful. So they reset their goal to the higher one, but when they reach that goal, they see that there's still more they can do, and so they reset their goal again…and again…and again. They never arrive at their destination, and that means they also never have the peace of mind or satisfaction of completing a task and doing it well. This is sometimes called *goal-vaulting* because they vault over one goal to a higher one over and over again.

Perfectionism can be debilitating because it prevents happiness and contentment. Kids who struggle with perfectionism often under-perform, under-sell themselves, and don't feel good even when they accomplish their goals. They may also over-perform (always at the highest level) and still not feel good. Do you ever find yourself not believing your parents and teachers when they tell you that you've done a great job? If so, it may be because the Worry Monster (with his friend the Perfectionist Monster) is telling you that you're not good enough or that you need to do more. Perfectionists tend to focus on the one thing they did wrong rather than all of the things they did right. They also tend to notice when someone is better than they are at something, and then they think of themselves as failures.

> *I compare myself to others who are much more experienced than I am, and I become frustrated that I am not at the same level as they are.*
>
> ~ 15-year-old warrior

Eating Disorders

Individuals who are perfectionistic and high-achieving seem to be at greater risk for eating disorders. Eating disorders are not often talked about when people talk about anxiety; however, they are anxiety disorders too and can become dangerous and even life-threatening if they aren't treated. Eating disorders all involve an obsessive or intense need to have one's body look a certain way—generally more "perfect." This fear changes the way a person thinks, the way a person sees him- or herself in the mirror, and the way a person thinks about food and eating (and yes, eating disorders affect boys, too).

> *Paul is overly concerned about his body image and health. He runs two times a day and counts his calories. If he doesn't run two times or goes over his calorie intake goal, he feels bad about himself and is preoccupied until he runs extra miles the next day. Paul fears that if he doesn't carefully control every calorie he eats or expends, he will wake up with his life/body out of control.*

Sometimes people who have anxiety try to eat "really healthy" because they are afraid that if they don't, not only will they get fat, but they also might get sick. These people are less concerned about their weight and appearance and more afraid of losing control of what is happening in their body.

If you think you have an eating disorder, remember that it's really, really hard to battle it all by yourself. The best thing to do is to tell your parents or a trusted adult that you have a problem, and they can get you the support you need so that you can feel better about how you take care of your body. Starving yourself is *not* taking care of yourself. Overeating, feeling guilty about what you ate, and then trying really hard to make up for what you ate by not eating anything later or exercising really hard is *not* taking care of yourself. And if you don't take care of your body, then your awesome brain can't do all of the great things it will be able to do if it gets the right amount of nutritious food to keep it running properly. So if you are having trouble with an eating disorder (or think you may be having trouble), don't hide it, and don't tackle it alone. In fact, trying to hide or cover up problems is the kind of behavior that the Worry Monster loves to see! It's worse for him—and better for you—if you have some help.

What If This Stuff Describes You?

Now you know about all of the different types of worries and fears that the Worry Monster uses to make people feel bad. You may feel that one or more of the things on the list applies to you. It's important to know that many people have some of the thoughts and behaviors listed in this chapter, but that doesn't necessarily mean they have an actual problem. For example, being a "neat freak" does not mean you have OCD. Trying to do a good job doesn't mean you are a perfectionist. And not eating sugary desserts after every dinner doesn't mean you have an eating disorder. Sometimes when we do stuff like that, its actually healthier. And some of the things we do are just quirky and weird. Is it okay to be weird? *Of course it is!* Our weirdnesses make us interesting!

I certainly do not want you to think that there is something wrong with you just because you do some of the things you just read about. In fact, even if you think you really do have one or more of the types of worries or fears listed in this chapter, that still doesn't mean there's anything wrong with you. It just means that you have the Worry Monster following you around, bullying you into doing things that don't let you live as happily and contentedly as you could be living. And there's something we can do about that!

If you think that you experience anything you read about here, please don't hesitate to tell your parents or another trusted adult about it. Remember, the Worry Monster does not want you to talk about him to anyone else, which is exactly why you need to. If worry and fear are having a significant effect on your ability to feel happy and to go to normal events like school and social gatherings, then it's pretty likely that the Worry Monster is messing with you. The tools in this book may be enough to help you get rid of him, but these skills can also support work that you may be doing with a counselor or therapist. You do not need to fight the Worry Monster alone. Admitting you could use some help and support and then getting help are signs of maturity and characteristics of successful people.

What Does Anxiety Look and Feel Like?

Okay, now you know about how anxiety works in our brain and body, and you know the types of anxiety that you can experience. We are getting closer to putting together our battle plan for fighting the Worry Monster. But first, let's take an even closer look at how anxiety can look and feel when the Worry Monster is bullying you.

So what does anxiety look like? Think back to all of the those body symptoms that excessive amounts of adrenaline cause when blood leaves your main organs in order to make you into a "super fighter or flighter." Now let's put those symptoms into everyday settings.

Often people who are feeling anxious aren't sure what to call it; they may not even realize that they are feeling anxious. Some people complain of having headaches and/or stomachaches in the morning before school, before a birthday party, before a test, and/or before bedtime. They may have trouble relaxing, have low energy, have trouble sleeping, have to go to the bathroom all the time, and may not have much of an appetite. There are plenty of other anxiety-related behaviors, too. These include nail biting, picking at one's skin, sucking on t-shirts, eating non-food items like napkins or ice, extreme clinginess, holding in one's bowels, and an excessive need for reassurance ("Did I do it right?" "Are you going to be okay?" "Am I going to be okay?").

Activity: Do you experience any of these body feelings? What do you do when you feel them? Think about the things you do when you are worried or scared. Do you bite your nails, ask lots of questions, get quiet, cry, yell, run away, get headaches, or experience stomachaches? Identify your worry indicators so that you will be able to tell when the Worry Monster is trying to trick you and make you worry about something.

Avoidance

In addition to physical complaints, you might find yourself doing something very common among people who worry or are afraid of something—and that is avoiding it, or ignoring it, or pretending it isn't there. Avoidance is the Worry Monster's best friend. The more a person avoids a certain situation, the stronger his worry and anxiety about it get. It's that simple. We avoid what we don't like. If you don't like to fly, you take the extra time it takes to get to your destination by driving. If you don't like animals, you don't go to the zoo. If you're afraid of insects, you don't go outdoors very often. Avoidance is a natural human response. However, it can get in the way of living a satisfying and fulfilling life. Some people end up avoiding regular life activities like going to school, talking to people, trying new things, taking a risk, and getting in front of people—all regular life activities. Avoiding things may also cause you to quit something you love to do, like art or music or sports, or not get to know other kids because of worry and fear of being rejected or saying something embarrassing.

> *Activity: What do you avoid? Think about the things that you don't like to do and try to get out of doing. Write them down on a piece of paper, and then write why you don't like doing them. Try to see if any of the things on your avoidance list are due to worrying or being scared of what might happen or how you might perform. This will help you uncover where the Worry Monster may be quietly bullying you.*

You will be learning ways to *face* the Worry Monster and gain victories over him because *avoiding* him only makes the Worry

Monster stronger. For example, if you refuse to go to birthday parties or other social events because you are afraid of what might happen, continuing to avoid parties just supports the notion that something bad will happen. Like I said, avoidance is the Worry Monster's best friend since he helps the Worry Monster's lies seem true.

Besides avoidance, people with anxiety sometimes do things that are considered "acting out" when really they are just plain scared. These behaviors may include crying, meltdowns, or other disruptive behavior. Do you ever get mad and lash out when you are actually scared? You know, like yell at your sister because she touched your half of the car seat? If you do, there is nothing wrong with you. It just means that the Worry Monster is getting to you. It probably also means that you may be misunderstood because you are seen as being difficult and oppositional (*oppositional* is a word parents and doctors use to describe children who don't do things the way parents want them to). If I am describing you, it is because your amygdala, or your "emotional brain," is overriding your thinking brain. You likely are not able to think clearly when you are scared, and you may react by refusing, running away, ripping up paper, hitting, pushing, and/or screaming. If these behaviors sometimes apply to you, the tools you will learn in this book will help you to stop doing them.

> *It's weird. Some kids melt down both at school and at home. Some just melt down at school, and some just melt down at home. I try not to show my feelings at school. I wait until I get home.*
>
> ~ eight-year-old warrior

Whether you are experiencing strong body symptoms related to excessive adrenaline (stomach pain, headaches, chest tightening) or are refusing to participate in an activity to avoid these uncomfortable feelings, remember that anxious and uncomfortable feelings *always* go away eventually. Even the really bad feelings *always* go away. It doesn't feel like it when it is happening, but they *always* do.

Sometimes we just need to get through the bad feelings. Surviving the Worry Monster's attack is a victory in itself.

I know that you may not be able to find words to describe your experience to your parents when you are worried or scared. All you can do is try. Do your best to tell your parents when you are nervous, worried, or scared. This will help you get through the difficult feelings and also will weaken the Worry Monster's power.

Things to Remember

- ✔ There are several different types of anxiety that the Worry Monster uses to bully you.

- ✔ People show their worry or fear in physical symptoms or behaviors or both. The symptoms and behaviors can be quiet ones, or they can be loud.

- ✔ Avoidance is a common behavior when you are worried or scared.

- ✔ Anxious feelings *always* go away eventually.

- ✔ Tell your parents or another trusted adult when you are feeling worried or scared.

CHAPTER 4

Cognitive (Thinking) Model of Anxiety

When we fill our thoughts with right things, the wrong ones have no room to enter.

~ Joyce Meyer

The cognitive, or thinking, model of anxiety is considered a highly effective approach to understanding and dealing with anxiety and the Worry Monster. Going back to our brains, our thinking (or *cognition*) comes from our frontal lobes—the part of the brain where we do most of our thinking. Our frontal lobes are the front portion of our brain behind our forehead and eyes. The reason we are "masters of the universe" is because we have very big frontal lobes that allow us to problem solve—more so than any other species. You have already learned that we need our amygdala to stay alive, but most of the time when it is "turned on" we don't need it to be on because we are merely nervous, worried, scared, or because we need to perform, go someplace new, leave a parent, or do any of number of other things the Worry Monster can bully us about.

Thoughts Cause Feelings

Our thoughts, behaviors, and feelings are all connected. So if we change our thinking, it leads to changes in our behaviors and feelings. Similarly, if we change our behaviors, it leads to changes in our thinking and feelings. For example, if I am *worried* (feeling) about going to a party because I don't know who is going to be there, I may be *thinking* (thought) a worrisome thought like, "I won't have anyone to talk to." I then may have an *upset stomach* and a little *headache*, and finally I decide I want to *avoid* the party (behavior). On the other hand, if I tell myself that I know that some people from my class will be there (thought), my stomachache and headache may go away, I will feel less worried (feeling), and I will be more likely to go to the party (behavior). Make sense?

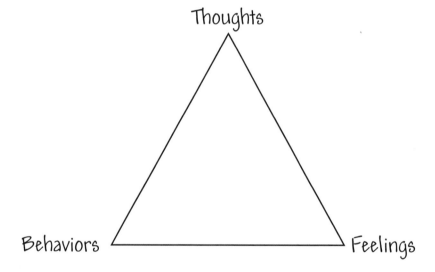

The main concept in the cognitive model of anxiety (the thinking model of anxiety) is that our *thoughts* are always responsible for our *feelings*. Our irrational and worried thoughts are almost always exaggerations of what could be or what might be, and they usually sound like this: "What if I...?" "What if you...?" "What if they...?" "What's going to happen to her if she doesn't...?" "How am I ever going to...?" "What will people think if...?" These are all future-based thoughts that trigger our amygdala to make us feel uncomfortable, worried, and scared.

How the Worry Monster Works

So here is how the Worry Monster works. You have a troubling thought: "Oh my gosh, my mom is going to leave, and she's never coming back." Your amygdala goes off, and your inner alarm bells start ringing. Body symptoms quickly follow—you may have an upset stomach and a tight chest, feel light-headed, and have tingling in your fingers. You then have more thoughts about what additional bad things that are going to happen after the first bad things start happening and how everything is awful.

All of this is going on inside your head, and so you say something like, "I'm not going to that party," or "I'm not going to that school." Meanwhile you may be crying, screaming, hiding, and/or being behaviorally disruptive, rude, and/or oppositional. Don't be embarrassed. These are all responses to feeling scared, worried, and anxious. The Worry Monster is definitely messing with you at this point.

Here Comes Adrenaline!

Every time the Worry Monster gives you a worrisome or scary thought, your amygdala activates and sends a message through your body that says: "Get me more adrenaline, quick!" So, for example, if you are going to take a test and you think, "Oh my gosh! I'm going to forget everything that I studied last night and do badly on the test," then squirt goes the adrenaline, flooding through your body. "Oh my gosh! I'm going to *fail* this test," and your body squirts more adrenaline. "Oh no, my parents are going to be *so mad* at me," and another squirt, even more adrenaline. "I'm not going get on the honor roll," new squirt. "Oh my gosh! I'm going to have to miss my…," squirt, squirt, squirt; it just keeps going and going and going. Think of a squirt gun squirting water every time you think another worrisome thought. This is like adrenaline squirting through our bodies.[10] The more adrenaline that moves through our bodies, the more we are being activated to fight or run away—which is not going to be helpful when we are taking a test.

Activity: Where Do You Feel It?

You can tell when the Worry Monster is visiting you by paying attention to your body. Ask yourself these questions:

✔ How do I feel when I am worried or scared?

✔ Where do I feel it in my body? Does my head hurt? Do I feel dizzy? Does my stomach feel funny or nauseous? Am I breathing faster? Do I feel out of breath?

When you have answered these questions, you have gotten in touch with your body, and you now know how to tell when the Worry Monster is bullying you.

Taking on the Worry Monster

So how do you handle the Worry Monster? Taming and getting rid of him is a team effort. You are going to gang up on him with your parents and/or other trusted adults. You can also do it alone if you feel strongly about wanting to defeat him by yourself. You are going to face the Worry Monster and your fears and worries. Remember, avoiding what you are scared of only makes the Worry Monster stronger. Each time you face the Worry Monster, he gets smaller and less powerful. It takes a lot of courage to face your fears and worries. Be patient with yourself, and encourage yourself. You can even reward yourself with each victory you get by doing something nice for yourself. Or, if your parents are helping you with your worries, they can set up a reward system for you. Maybe each time you get a victory, they will buy you a milkshake, or take you to a movie you want to see, or something like that that you can agree on. The rewards are just a way of letting you know that beating the Worry Monster is something to celebrate. Each time you tell the Worry Monster to take a hike and leave you alone, you will be getting stronger and feeling more confident. You can do this!

Things to Remember

- ✔ Our worrisome thoughts trigger our amygdala to release adrenaline.

- ✔ Too much adrenaline makes our bodies feel scared.

- ✔ Our thoughts affect our feelings and behaviors.

- ✔ The more we think worrisome thoughts, the more adrenaline is released, and the more scared our bodies feel.

- ✔ Changing our thoughts changes our feelings and behaviors—and sends the Worry Monster away.

- ✔ Facing your worry and fear is critical for making them go away.

- ✔ You can do this!

CHAPTER 5

Thinking Errors

You wouldn't worry so much about what others think of you if you realized how seldom they do.

~ Eleanor Roosevelt

As we have discussed, the Worry Monster places worrisome and irrational (not true) thoughts into our brains to make us feel worried and scared. While these thoughts may seem random, they actually have some predictable patterns that are sometimes referred to as thinking errors, or "stinking thinking." Becoming aware of the types of thinking errors in general, and your personal thinking errors in particular, can help you better understand how the Worry Monster makes you have uncomfortable feelings. In other words, what is the Worry Monster telling you to make you worried and scared?

This chapter discusses the most commonly identified thinking errors.[11] You don't have to memorize these. If fact, you can still defeat the Worry Monster even if you don't know what type of thinking errors the Worry Monster uses against you. Feel free to skip this part and go to the next chapter if this is more detail than you need. However, some people find it helpful to understand the tactics that the Worry Monster uses, especially the last two: "What if…?" and "What will people think…?"

Catastrophizing

Many people who get visits from the Worry Monster tend to exaggerate and turn their worries into catastrophes. They may think that disaster will strike at any time, that the worst possibilities are going to happen, and that they won't be able to handle it when those bad things do happen. "If I don't do well on this spelling test, I'm never going to get into college!" "I will never have any friends!" "Mom is five minutes late already—I'm sure she's gotten into a horrible car accident! How will my life change if I don't have a mom?" A person who thinks like this jumps from feeling a small worry to imagining a total catastrophe.

All or Nothing Thinking

This kind of thinking is also called black and white thinking because there is no middle ground, no gray area. It's an inflexible and irrational style of thinking because it implies that no middle ground exists between extremes; it is "always" or "never." It is extreme thinking—that we either have to do things perfectly or have failed, that people either like us or hate us. Lots of kids use all or nothing thinking when they think about their grades. To people with this thinking error, only an A is success; any other grade is failure—even a B, even though we all know that a B is still considered above average.

Filtering

Filtering means focusing on the negative aspects of a situation while ignoring the positive parts. For example, let's say you got invited to a party you wanted to go to, but once you get home, you only focus on the times at the party when you didn't feel included. Or even though you had a lot of fun at the school picnic, you only think about the part of the picnic when the kid in front of you took the last bag of Doritos and you had to have plain potato chips. It doesn't matter that the party or the picnic was fun for most of the time you were there; all that you can seem to focus on is the one small thing that happened that wasn't as good as everything else.

Selective Attention

Selective attention is similar to filtering. It's when you look for aspects of a situation that are consistent with and confirm your beliefs about something while at the same time ignoring information that goes against what you know to be true. Someone with selective attention might say, "My coach thinks I didn't play well and that I need to work harder," when in fact the coach actually made several positive comments and offered constructive criticism about only one play the person made. Or someone might say, "I can't believe I missed that question! How stupid can I be?!" in response to missing one out of 100 questions on a test. Remember, there will always be someone smarter, dumber, taller, shorter, more athletic, clumsier, richer, poorer, prettier, or uglier than you. There is no such thing as *the* best there is—only *your* best.

Magnifying

Magnifying means blowing something out of proportion or making something seem bigger and worse than it really is—for example, "I made a mistake, and now everyone is going to laugh at me every time they see me," or, "I failed the test, and now my future is ruined!" or, "When I was giving my presentation to the class, I dropped my pen, and now everyone thinks I am clumsy and stupid. And they won't want me to play kickball with them ever again." Magnifying is a lot like catastrophizing; it's making a whole lot out of almost nothing. Think about it: Does anyone care if you made a mistake? Probably not. Will one bad test really ruin your future? That's pretty doubtful. Did anyone even notice that you dropped your pen during your presentation? Highly unlikely, and even if they did, they've probably forgotten it already. People don't notice what you do nearly as much as *you* notice what you do!

Shoulds

This thinking error refers to "rules" that some people have about how things should be. The rules might be about their home, their school, or the entire world, and they are identifiable when we use words like *should*, *have to*, and *must* to explain how things "should" and "must" be. "I should not make mistakes." "I have to always do things perfectly." "I must always get 100% on tests." "I must know more than everyone else." Also, "would haves" and "could haves" create uncomfortable feelings that can make us feel sad or depressed for hours, days, months, or even years. "I would have gotten an A if the teacher hadn't put in a trick question." "I could have been the top speller, but I got a really hard word." "I could have gotten first place, but I let Jason win." Watch out for "shoulda…woulda…coulda…"!

Mind Reading

Mind reading is what you do when you think you know what others are thinking—particularly when it comes to what they are thinking about *you*. Of course, we almost never think that people are thinking good things about us. Instead, it's always negative and bad. "They think I'm stupid." "They don't want me to play with them." "I can tell you think I'm a bad singer, Mom. You keep saying nice things, but you don't really mean it." "I can tell you're mad because you keep reading the paper and ignoring me."

But let's face it: if you were an excellent mind reader, then you would use your powers to find out what the teacher was going to put on the test so you could look up the answers ahead of time, right? And you would know what your parents were going to give you for your birthday before you opened your presents, right? But you don't know these things because you can't read people's minds, and so you can't assume that you know what they think about you either.

Personalizing

Personalizing is what you do when you assume that something that happened was because of you. When you personalize, you make everything about yourself, when most things actually have nothing to do with you. For example, your friend cancels plans to get together, and you assume, "She doesn't like me anymore." In fact, your friend actually canceled because her parents decided that the family needed to go check on a relative who was just involved in an accident. The situation has nothing to do with you, but you assume that it does.

Overgeneralizing

Looking at one situation or incident and thinking that it will always be that way or happen that way again is overgeneralizing. Once something happens, you assume that it will always happen the same way each time. "I didn't get invited to Bryan's party. I'm never going to get invited to anyone's party again!" "I got a C on that test. I'm just stupid, and I'm never going to do well on a test again." *Always, never, only, every, all, none, everyone, no one,* and *nothing* are danger words. Use them with care!

Probability Overestimation

Probability overestimation is similar to magnifying and catastrophizing—it's worrying about something that actually has a slim chance of occurring. If you look at the actual facts and statistics, the thing you fear is easily proven to be unlikely to happen. However, even the small and extremely remote possibility of the accident or incident occurring seems scary. "The plane could crash, and I will die," "I might get kidnapped," "My parents could get killed," and "A meteor might fall on me" are all examples of probability overestimation. Fortunately, these events rarely occur, but you react to them as though they are very likely to happen. Another example of probability overestimation is when you're afraid that you might fail a test, even though you studied and have never failed a test before. Could it happen? Sure. Is it likely to happen? Absolutely not!

Additional Thinking Errors

Two other common thinking errors are "What if...?" and "What will people think...?"[12] Think about how many times you say these phrases and how they make you doubt yourself and worry

about what will happen in the future. You can't control what people think; you can only control yourself, so worrying about what others might think doesn't help you. It *does* help, however, to remember that you probably don't spend much time wondering why other people do the things they do, do you? So it's pretty likely that they aren't paying too much attention to what you do either.

"What if…?"

The "What ifs" may be the most single powerful trick the Worry Monster uses. The Worry Monster can put a "What if" in front of anything:

- ✔ "What if I don't get the part I want in the play?"
- ✔ "What if I don't get on the team?"
- ✔ "What if I do badly on the test?"
- ✔ "What if I don't get invited to the party?"
- ✔ "What if I get scared and want to come home early?"

And the list goes on and on and on. Any time you say, "What if…?" to yourself or others, it means the Worry Monster is probably at work. Knowing how the Worry Monster uses the "What if…?" strategy against her, a brave 13-year-old warrior I know now says, "What if? Whatever!" and just dismisses the Worry Monster like he doesn't matter to her one bit. And it works!

"What will people think…?"

"What will people think…?" is a perfect companion to "What if…?" With both of these tactics, the Worry Monster has the fear market cornered. Once he tells you about all of the possible things that can go wrong with your life using the "What ifs…?" he then follows up with "And what will people think…?"

- ✔ "What will people think of me if I forget my lines?"
- ✔ "What will people think if I strike out?"
- ✔ "What will people think if I don't get an A?"
- ✔ "What will people think if I'm the only one not invited?"
- ✔ "What will people think if I go home early?"

The Short List

There are a lot of thinking errors listed in this chapter, and if it feels like it's too much to remember, here's a list that is much shorter. All of the different thinking errors fall into two main categories: (1) jumping to conclusions about bad things that might happen, and (2) thinking that things are worse than they really are.[13] You will find that these categories cover just about every kind of worried thinking you could possibly have.

Are you starting to get annoyed with the Worry Monster? I certainly am. All he does is make us miserable! And he does this simply by messing with our thinking so our alarm bells go off, our body gets flooded with adrenalin, and—no surprise—we feel awful. Enough is enough!

Activity: What Are Your Thinking Patterns?

This activity is designed to help you become familiar with the types of thinking errors you might engage in. You may find that you use the same thinking errors over and over, or you might discover that you have a variety of thinking errors. You can do this activity by yourself or with an adult. Try to identify the type of thinking error associated with each statement. You can find the answers on page 51.

1. *They think I'm stupid.*

2. *I never do things right. I always blow it!*

3. *I never get picked to be a partner.*

4. *I shouldn't make any mistakes.*

5. *What will people think if I mess up?*

6. *I know the teacher said I did a good job, but she corrected two of my answers, so she really didn't mean it.*

7. *I can't go on the fieldtrip without you. What if I get lost and they leave without me?*

8. *What if burglars break into my house and take me?*

9. *They wouldn't let me lead the line walking into the museum, so the whole fieldtrip was ruined.*

10. *I know she said she liked what I was wearing, but she was laughing with Julie after she looked at me.*

11. *If I don't get a good grade on this, I will never get into college.*

12. *She cancelled the party because she didn't want me there.*

So how did you do? Many of the statements could fall into several categories of thinking errors. The main point is that you can learn to identify your thinking errors and see how the Worry Monster tricks you into being worried and scared. Look out, Worry Monster; you are going to become weaker and weaker until you totally lose your power!

Things to Remember

- ✔ Our worrisome thoughts are always responsible for feelings of worry and fear.

- ✔ The Worry Monster uses several different kinds of thinking tricks to make us worry and feel scared.

- ✔ People tend to have a few "favorite" thinking errors that often make them worry or feel scared.

- ✔ The Worry Monster is *always* lying to you!

Things to Do

- ✔ Identify your thinking errors.

- ✔ Ask yourself, "What does the Worry Monster tell me to make me feel worried and scared?"

- ✔ Smile, because you are starting to outsmart the Worry Monster.

Thinking Patterns Activity Answers

1. Mind Reading
2. All or Nothing Thinking, Magnifying, Overgeneralizing
3. All or Nothing Thinking, Magnifying, Overgeneralizing, Personalizing
4. Shoulds
5. "What will people think...?"
6. Selective Attention
7. Catastrophizing, "What if...?"
8. Catastrophizing, Probability Overestimation, "What if...?"
9. Filtering
10. Selective Attention, Personalizing
11. Catastrophizing
12. Personalizing

CHAPTER 6

Cognitive (Thinking) Strategies

You don't have to control your thoughts. You just have to stop letting them control you.

~ Dan Millman

Now we are getting to the really exciting part; the part where we start to take charge of the Worry Monster by using his own sneaky strategies against him! He hates it when we realize that he is there, and even more when we know how he works. Unfortunately, most people never learn the simple fact that our *thoughts* determine our *feelings* and our *behaviors*.[14] So you already know more about this than most adults do. It's true!

You now know that when you are feeling scared, you are thinking a certain way that is responsible for your awful anxious feelings and behaviors. So the first thing you can do to start the process of chasing the Worry Monster away is to ask yourself, "What am I thinking right now?" Some people can answer this question easily, while others have trouble identifying what they are thinking. Even if you have trouble figuring out what you are thinking because your body feelings are so strong, keep trying. With practice, most people eventually figure out at least one thing the Worry Monster is telling them. Also, you are going to learn about several things you can do to practice chasing the Worry Monster away. These strategies will involve your *behavior* instead of your *thinking*. People of all ages, not just kids, have trouble identifying what they are thinking and feeling. That is why we have multiple ways to successfully make the Worry Monster go away and stay away.

Four Steps

The approach we will take is really very simple. You are going to become a detective in order to figure out what the Worry Monster is telling you and making you think. The way to do this is to learn to follow four simple steps to chase the Worry Monster away:

- ✔ *Identify the thought*: "What am I thinking about? What is my thinking error? Is it that I'm scared I'm going to fail the test?"

- ✔ *Challenge the thought*: "Is it true that I always fail? Do I have evidence to support that I always fail?"

- ✔ *Modify the thought*: "The test is going to be hard, but I am prepared. I usually get nervous before math tests but generally do pretty well."

- ✔ *Replace the thought*: "I am prepared. I will try my best and will do fine."

In this simple four-step model, you will become aware of your worrisome and untrue thought so you can turn down the volume of your small amygdala (your emotional brain) and turn up the power of your big frontal lobes (your thinking brain). This way, the warning signals from your amygdala will decrease, the adrenaline squirts will go away, and blood will stay in your brain. Keeping blood in your brain is what you need to fight the Worry Monster.

Remember, you can do this with your parents or a trusted adult, especially when you are just getting used to thinking this way. Over time, you will find that this way of thinking will become natural to you, and you'll be able to do it on your own. You will be asking yourself simple questions like, "What am I thinking? What is the Worry Monster telling me? Is this thought true? Can I prove it? Can I prove that something's going to happen to me? Can I prove that I am going to fail the test? Can I prove that no one's going to like me?"

The Worry Monster puts these worrisome thoughts in our head, and we need to challenge them. Think to yourself, "How can I look at this differently?" Here's an example. You may be scared to go to a party because you think the people there won't be nice to you. But then you think: "When I go to a party, most of the kids will probably be nice to me, and maybe one or two might not be very nice, but isn't that normal? What are some other times I was worried about going to a party and it worked out fine?"

As we have discussed, changing your thinking will result in having different feelings and different behaviors. We will have negative and distressing feelings if we are thinking, "Everyone hates me," "I'm going to fail," "My teacher is going to be mad at me," "My parents are going to ground me," "I'm never going to amount to anything," "I'm too fat," or "I'm stupid." However, we will have more positive and less distressing feelings if we learn to replace those negative thoughts with healthier ones. For instance, how about changing those thoughts to: "I have friends, which means some people like me," "I studied for the test, so I probably will do okay," "My teacher just wants me to do my best," "I can handle it if my parents ground me; it's not the end of the world," "I'm going to take one day at a time," "I am fine the way I am," or "I don't like making mistakes, but they happen sometimes." These healthier, more positive thoughts are the thoughts the Worry Monster hates most. He hates it when we know he is there and when we come up with rational thoughts by using our big thinking brains. He's counting on us believing his lying, sneaky, mean, and manipulative thoughts, no matter how ridiculous they may be.

So that's all we need to do to with our thinking: *identify* it, *challenge* it, *modify* it, and then *replace* it. It's a four-step model that you do over and over again until you feel bored with doing it because you don't need to do it anymore.

Here is an example of a warrior named Adam. It shows how Adam's father helped him work through his worries by using this four-step approach to change his thinking. Adam was new to this approach, so he wasn't able to talk himself through his fear yet.

Adam, age eight, doesn't want to go to soccer tryouts, even though he loves soccer and his friends will be there. He starts to protest several days before, saying, "I am not going, and you can't make me." His father is used to this kind of anxious response from Adam.

Father: *It sounds like the Worry Monster is visiting you again.*

Adam: *No, he's not. I just don't want to go.*

Father: *Hmm, let's see. I know you love soccer and want to be on your friends' team again. I'm guessing the Worry Monster is trying to trick you. Remember when he did that to you before last year's tryouts?*

Adam: *Yeah, it wasn't as bad as I thought it was going to be.*

Father: *Where is the Worry Monster making you feel bad in your body? Is he making your heart beat fast, giving you a stomachache, or making you feel dizzy?*

Adam: *He's making my chest feel funny, and I can't breathe right.*

Father: *Remember what we learned about the survival response? When the Worry Monster tells us scary things, it makes our body feel like we need to fight or run. What might the Worry Monster be telling you about this tryout? I'm guessing he might be saying something like, "What if you make a mistake? What will people think? People are going to be watching you." Is he saying something like that?*

Adam: *He's telling me that I might not know where to go when I get there, and I might forget how to kick and dribble.*

Father: *I figured he was telling you something like that because I know how much you like soccer, so it would have to be something pretty bad for you to not want to go try out for the team. You know how the Worry Monster tells you lies to make your worried and scared. Now that we know what he's saying to you, what's the evidence that what he's saying is true? What can you tell him to make him stop? How can you think differently?*

Adam: *I can tell myself that I know where to go because I've been there before. I can also tell him that I know he's lying because I play soccer a lot and know how to play.*

Father: *Do you feel scared when you think those thoughts?*

Adam: *No, but he makes me feel bad when he tells me the other stuff.*

Father: *I know. How about we do this: Tryouts are still a few days away. So during that time, you tell me when he's making you feel bad, and then we can talk about the lies he's telling you and talk back to him with the truth. Do you think we can try that?*

Adam: *Okay. We can do that. You're still going to stay the whole time I'm at tryouts, right?*

Father: *Right.*

Adam eventually learned to recognize when the Worry Monster was visiting, and he became good at identifying the worrisome thoughts that were making him scared. He also learned to challenge his thinking on his own. He talked to his dad about it after he made the Worry Monster go away, as well as when the

Worry Monster was being a super-bully and wouldn't go away. Adam and his father became a good team united to defeat the Worry Monster!

An Example of When I Changed My Thinking

You may be surprised to learn that the Worry Monster still visits me sometimes. In fact, the Worry Monster came to visit me when I started to write this book! I had planned to write the book for several years. I had so many ideas to share, and I felt that the words would come rather easily because I would simply be writing about the work I do day in and day out, as well as speak about regularly. I finally planned a weekend away for intensive writing and was getting excited as the days approached. It was the Friday before the writing weekend, and guess who came to visit?

It started slowly on Friday with a little pressure in my chest and an uneasy feeling in my stomach. I shook it off and did a pretty good job of ignoring it, and I was able to focus on my clients. I came home to pack clothes for the weekend, and the weird feeling was still there. The feeling grew on the drive to my destination and remained steady until bedtime. "Ah ha!" said the Worry Monster as I laid in bed trying to fall asleep, "It's time to attack!" And boy did he attack.

The negative thoughts came fast. "What if you don't have anything to say? What if you don't get enough done? What if you have trouble writing what you want to say? Maybe you don't know as much as you think you do." As these thoughts were running through my mind, I became very aware of the feelings that I'd been experiencing in my chest and stomach all day.

Believe it or not, I actually smiled and thought, "How funny. The Worry Monster is coming to visit me when I am preparing to write about how to get rid of him." As you know, the Worry Monster and I are pretty well-acquainted. We're not exactly best friends, but we know each other well. I took a deep breath, and then several more, and asked myself, "What am I thinking?" It was not hard to identify my thoughts. I made a mental list and then set out to change them.

Here is what my list looked like (in my mind):

Worry Monster Thought	My New Thought
"What if you don't have anything to say?"	"I always have something to say about the Worry Monster."
"What if you don't get enough done?"	"I will take one step at a time and do as much as I can."
"What if you have trouble writing what you want to say?"	"I will focus on my ideas and experiences."
"Maybe you don't know as much as you think you do."	"I have been doing this work for a long time and know enough to share my experiences with others."

As I was going through and changing my thinking, the pressure in my chest started to go away, as well as the uneasy feeling in my stomach. Once again, I was reminded how sneakily the Worry Monster works, and also how simple it is to make him go away.

Additional Cognitive (Thinking) Strategies

Positive Self-Talk

In addition to the simple four-step model, a great way of defeating the Worry Monster is through positive self-talk. Positive self-talk is one of the oldest sure-fire strategies around. One well-known example of it is in the children's book *The Little Engine that Could*, in which the small engine said, "I think I can, I think I can, I think I can" as she delivered toys to the girls and boys on the other side of the mountain. That's the kind of self-talk that encourages us and makes us strong.

Here's another example of positive self-talk that you may have done many times in your life.[15] It is the middle of the night, and it's dark, and you walk down the hallway saying, "I'm not afraid,

I'm not afraid, I'm not afraid, I'm not afraid." This simple strategy works because you are using your thinking brain to turn off your amygdala. If you did not take over the command center in your brain, the Worry Monster would activate your amygdala by making you say something different—something scarier—like, "Oh no, I'm going to be attacked by a ghost, I'm going to be attacked by a ghost, I'm going to be attacked by a ghost!" I know; it sounds way too simple, but it works. Changing your thinking or talking yourself into feeling brave changes the way you feel and chases the Worry Monster away!

> *I always get afraid when I walk into a new situation where I don't know who is going to be there. My heart starts pounding, and I start to feel a little dizzy. I try to remember to say the same thing to myself over and over until my heart starts to slow down. Lately, I say, "Nothing bad is going to happen, nothing bad is going to happen, nothing bad is going to happen."*
>
> *I am getting used to the idea that the Worry Monster comes to visit me at certain times. One of his favorite times is when I read the first question of a test. If I don't know the answer right away, he tells me, "You are going to fail." I have learned to say back to him, "I will be fine." I say it over and over and over until I am able to focus on the test question instead of him.*
>
> 12-year-old warrior

Worry Time

Scheduling "worry time" is a great way to put some boundaries on our worry.[16] It also allows us to not get bogged down by the Worry Monster because we can tell ourselves, "I don't have to worry about that now; worry time is from 7:45 to 8:00 tonight." Worry time not only reduces worrying during the day, but it also reduces it overall because we often forget what we were worrying about earlier in the day.

Worry Box

I have seen great results when someone creates a "worry box." The worry box, which can be an artistic creation from something as simple as a shoebox, becomes a place where you can put pieces of paper on which you have written down your worries so that you no longer have to think about them. Some kids put their worry box under their beds; some put it in the closet. It is also fun—and useful—to look in the worry box every once in awhile to see if the things you put in there were worth worrying about. Of course, only do this for the things that are no longer worries or are small worries, as we certainly don't want to make the Worry Monster right! And if the Worry Monster was right that something bad happened… well, guess what? You survived it!

"And then what?"

I am a big fan of the "And then what?" strategy. Here's how it works. After you have a worrisome or scary thought, you ask, "And then what?" It goes like this: "I'm worried that I'll get a bad grade on my test. *And then what?* I will get a bad grade in my class. *And then what?* My parents will be mad. *And then what?* I'll get grounded. *And then what?* I won't be able to see my friends. *And then what?* I will miss out on a fun sleepover."

You see? This keeps going and going. The next thing you do is become a detective and ask yourself if any of what you said is actually true. Does one bad test performance equal a bad grade in a class? Will your parents really ground you if you get a bad test grade or a bad grade in a class (when you are trying)? Will you really not be able to see your friends? As you can see, the "And then what?" technique is really good at uncovering lies the Worry Monster is telling you. You also will find out that you can handle most of the things the Worry Monster tells you, like missing a sleepover. So you missed it. So what?

Planning for Worst-Case Scenarios

Planning for worst-case scenarios is a good way to be prepared for what you are worrying about. As you have learned, we often have fears that we just accept instead of challenging how true they are. We also tend to feel that we won't be able to handle bad situations if and when they happen. Planning for worst-case scenarios means you think through how you will handle a situation if it were to come true. For example, I know a 10-year-old girl, Paige, who was worried that she wouldn't get the lead part in the play she was auditioning for, and it was very important to her. We used the worst-case scenario to work through this:

Paige: *I'm worried I won't get the lead part that I've been practicing for. Everyone expects me to get it, and I'll be disappointed and embarrassed if I don't get it.*

Me: *What will happen if you don't get the part?*

Paige: *I'll probably get another important role, just not the lead.*

Me: *What will happen then?*

Paige: *People may be a little surprised, but I'll work hard at my role and do the best I can.*

Me: *How will that be for you?*

Paige: *I guess it will be okay. I can try for the lead in the next play.*

Me: *So not getting the lead it is not as bad as you thought?*

Paige: *No, I guess not. It just felt like it would be.*

The worst-case scenario approach is another way of questioning the Worry Monster's lies, but your reasonable and rational thoughts are more powerful!

Things to Remember

✔ Our thoughts are responsible for our feelings and our behaviors.

✔ The Worry Monster tells us irrational and worrisome thoughts to make us feel worried and scared.

✔ We need to identify our thinking to help uncover what the Worry Monster is telling us.

✔ Not all kids, or even adults, can identify their thinking, but everyone can get better at it if they learn how.

✔ We can be detectives with our thoughts and ask ourselves if they are actually true.

✔ Changing our thoughts and replacing them with more reasonable ones turns our amygdala down and makes the Worry Monster weak and powerless.

✔ You have several different strategies to choose from to fight the Worry Monster.

✔ Your thinking brain is strong and powerful.

✔ You can do this!

CHAPTER 7

Mindfulness-Based
Interventions

The mind is everything. What you think, you become.
~ Buddha

I would like to introduce you to mindfulness-based strategies for fighting the Worry Monster. Mindfulness strategies come from Eastern philosophies, both Buddhist and Zen ways of thinking. The Dalai Lama, spiritual leader of Tibet and a very wise man, pointed out that people who live in the past tend to be depressed because it already happened and there's nothing they can do about it, and people who live in the future tend to be anxious because it hasn't happened yet and there's nothing they can do about it.[17] So if living in and thinking about the *past* makes us depressed, and living in and thinking about the *future* makes us anxious, then the goal is to try to live in the *present*. Simple to say, yet challenging to do.

Staying in the Present

In my own life, and through the experiences of many of my clients, I have learned that staying in the present is the single most powerful technique for keeping the Worry Monster at bay. Here's why: If we live in the present, everything is fine because most of the time, things are fine (or at least manageable enough) right at this moment. For example, right now, I am engaged in writing this book, and you are engaged in reading it. We are both hopefully engaged in something meaningful and are relaxed while doing it. You are learning about ways to fight the Worry Monster and are focusing on these words at this moment. Everything is fine right now.

But now let's decide it's time to start worrying—let's start to worry together. On your mark, get set, GO! Let's start thinking (worrying) about grades, upcoming tests, making the athletic team, getting invited to parties…. The list goes on and on and on about what we can choose to worry about right this second—and none of it has happened yet. Sorry to do that to you—to get your adrenalin going like that. I just needed to make the point about how easy it is to slide into worry about the future. Let's end that planned worrying exercise and come back to this book and the words you are reading. Bring your focus back to the present moment where everything was, and still is, fine.

Are you back to the present? It may take a moment. It can be hard to turn our amygdalas down and allow time for our blood to return to where it belongs. Give yourself some time. Take some deep breaths and return to these words when you are ready. Now, try to come back to the present moment where we are focused on doing our best and learning how to focus on the *present*. The Dalai Lama also says, "If the situation or problem is such that is can be remedied, there is no reason to worry about it. Alternatively, if there is no way out, no solution, no possibility of resolution, then there is also no point in being worried about it, because you can't do anything about it anyway."[18] Simply put, if you are worrying and there's something you can do about the situation, then do something about it, and stop worrying. If you are worrying and there's nothing you can do about it, then there's no point in worrying because there's nothing you can do about it. Yes, it can be hard to put these ideas into practice, but if we can nurture the mindset of living in the present right now, it can be highly effective in fighting the Worry Monster. However, this does *not* mean that you should go crazy over your spelling test and study for hours and hours or act out OCD rituals because you are "doing" something about what you are worrying about. It means that if you are worried that you upset your friend, ask her if you upset her rather than worrying about it for a week!

Of course, staying in the present is easier said than done. For example, last year doctors thought that my oldest daughter might have a serious medical condition. Part of the process of investigating the problem included my daughter seeing several specialists and having a brain x-ray. As you can imagine, the Worry Monster was spending a lot of time with me (at all hours of the day and night), telling me all of the awful things that could be diagnosed and all of the terrible future possibilities. I had to work very hard to stay focused in the present while reminding myself that we had several appointments scheduled and that we couldn't do anything more until we knew the facts. Fortunately, everything turned out fine. However, this serves as an example of how hard it was for me (an expert on banishing worry!) to try to stay in the present while acknowledging that there was nothing I could do about a potential problem that had yet to be discovered. And it also illustrates that I worried a lot over what turned out to be nothing.

This is also an example of how it is normal to be upset about scary things, but if we stay in the present, we can handle the scary stuff without getting overwhelmed. In my situation, I put all of my "What if's…?" on a list and then asked the doctors those questions when we had an appointment. I practiced breathing so I could stay calm and relax my body. I forced myself to tell the Worry Monster that I can handle whatever I have to do, and that lots of people get sick *and get better.*

> *I feel nervous on Sundays. I know the weekend is over, and I'm scared about going to school.*
>
> ~ nine-year-old warrior

The key point is that all worrisome problems live in the future, a time that has yet to exist. Thus, we can use our great thinking brains to solve any problem that occurs in the present, as opposed to worrying about every single problem before it actually happens in the future. Now it is true that we may be able to predict something in the future based on things that have already happened in the past. For instance, you might say, "I will get picked last at recess. I always do." Well, that may be true, but there's *still* nothing you can do about it *until* recess. If that's what is going to happen, then it is going to happen. You will have to deal with it later, and you *can* deal with it. Remember, you can put that worry in your handy dandy little worry box and pull it out another time (in the future). Should it ruin your day until then? Worrying about a future event doesn't do anything except make us miserable, cranky, and less able to think straight.

Here is an example of what we are talking about. I had a meeting with a seventh grader and her mother to work on fighting the Worry Monster. The girl's worry centered around schoolwork, test performance, and her fears of getting in trouble, even though in reality she never got in trouble—it was simply something she worried *might* happen one day. The Worry Monster was holding strong, and I was running out of ideas of how to support this teen in letting go of her worries. I was reviewing all of her worries in my head when suddenly it hit me! *They were all future-based.* When I told her this, she didn't believe me because her worries seemed so much in the present and right there in the room with us, like a bully breathing down her neck. I then listed them for her:

- ✔ "What if I do badly on the math test?"
- ✔ "What if I get caught talking in class?"
- ✔ "What if I don't make the soccer team?"
- ✔ "What if I don't get invited to the dance?"

As I continued to list them off, her eyes became as big as saucers. She sat quietly for some time. When she eventually spoke, she said, "Oh my gosh, it's true. None of them have happened yet!" I looked at her mother, who was sitting next to her. Her eyes were similarly wide open—like she was having her own "aha" moment. With a smile, she said, "I can't believe it. None of my own worries have happened yet either!"

So when you find yourself worrying, ask yourself what you are worrying about. Whether you know what the Worry Monster is telling you or not, try to focus on the present moment—right here, right now. It may take some practice to get the hang of this, but you will come to find that the present moment is almost always much better than the future worrisome one that hasn't yet occurred. If we expand our awareness at the present moment, we may realize that the sun is shining, or we are sitting with someone who cares about us, or our favorite song may be on the radio, or nature around us is especially beautiful today, or something nice may have happened an hour ago.

Letting Thoughts Pass

I want you to think about the image of King Kong on the top of a tall building swiping at fighter planes that are trying to destroy him. I like to use this image to represent how most of us approach our thinking: we often fight our thoughts. In addition, we often believe our own stinking thinking (which is what the Worry Monster wants us to do), even if the thinking is totally ridiculous, irrational, and not true!

Now I want you to visualize an airplane flying overhead pulling a banner that says, "Come join us at the county fair." You notice the plane and the banner as it is flying overhead, and then it is gone. About 10 minutes later, you notice the plane flying by again, and then again 10 minutes after that.

Eventually, the plane with its banner is gone, back to its hangar, and you forget that the plane and its banner ever existed. This is a metaphor for noticing our thinking and then letting our thoughts pass as if they don't much matter, like the banner advertising the county fair.

Mindfulness traditions suggest that our thoughts merely come to us, and who knows from where. So do we have to believe every irrational, worrisome, or scary thought the Worry Monster sends our way? No, we don't! We need to notice our thoughts and let them pass without getting so attached to them or rattled by them. A mentor of mine once taught me to say, "Hmm…, interesting…," following an unpleasant thought. It's a surprisingly simple yet effective technique of distancing yourself from the content of the thought. The next time you are thinking, "I am afraid my mom will not come back to pick me up," say to yourself, "Hmm…, that's interesting, because my mom always picks me up. She's never forgotten me once." You can even use a funny accent while saying this to further distance yourself from the scary thought—to ridicule it.

Controlling Your Breathing

Breathing is free, and we can breathe as much as we want. The air is free. And breathing takes no effort, at least if we're healthy. Breathing is an automatic ability we are born with, and it is a necessary process required for living. Breathing is also something we take for granted. We don't always appreciate how our breathing can help us, but we can use breathing as a powerful tool for calming ourselves during times of stress, worry, and fear. We can focus on our breathing, slow it down, and feel more relaxed as it slows down. A yoga instructor once told me that regular, slow, deep breathing actually tricks our mind into feeling calm. Conscious breathing allows oxygen to flow through our body and brain and counteracts feelings of stress and anxiety.

Remember what happens when our survival response is triggered? Blood leaves our brain and goes to our arms and legs so we can fight or run away. Deep breathing can keep our danger response from going off. It helps to keep blood in our brain and provides us with a feeling of relaxation.

> *My son developed an anxiety attack response to getting his blood pressure checked, which is something he had to do for his physicals for high school sports programs. I taught him how to focus on his breath while the cuff was on his arm, and it worked! He could get through having his blood pressure taken.*
>
> ~ father of a warrior

Activity: Belly Breathing

This is a very simple activity you can do by yourself or with your parents or family members. Find a comfortable place where you will not be interrupted. Lie down on your back, or sit on the floor yoga style, with your legs crossed in front of you. You can do the exercise sitting in a chair, too. It's something you can do just about anywhere. When you are ready to start, place your hands on your stomach. Keeping your hands on your stomach helps you check to make sure you are breathing deeply—not just through your chest, but through your belly. Belly breathing promotes relaxation, whereas breathing through your chest is associated with the survival response and running for your life (not relaxation!).

Take care to inhale slowly and then exhale slowly. You should feel your stomach muscles move up as you breathe in and down as you breathe out. Breathe through your nose, and be aware of the air moving in and out. Some yoga instructors suggest breathing in for the count of four seconds and then breathing out for the next four seconds. You can choose the number of seconds that feels comfortable for you. Some people like a four-count, others a six-count, while others prefer an eight-count. Again, do what feels right to you.

Ready to practice? We are going to start with a six-count and do it six times. Put your hands on your stomach. Ready? Here we go.

Slowly inhale 1-2-3-4-5-6; now slowly exhale 1-2-3-4-5-6.
Again, slowly inhale 1-2-3-4-5-6; slowly exhale 1-2-3-4-5-6.
Slowly inhale 1-2-3-4-5-6; now slowly exhale 1-2-3-4-5-6.
Again, slowly inhale 1-2-3-4-5-6; slowly exhale 1-2-3-4-5-6.
Slowly inhale 1-2-3-4-5-6; slowly exhale 1-2-3-4-5-6.
And last time, slowly inhale 1-2-3-4-5-6,
and now slowly exhale 1-2-3-4-5-6.

Are you more relaxed now than you were merely a minute ago? I am guessing that your answer is yes because this technique almost *always* works, at least in the present moment. Remember, deep breathing tricks our brain into feeling relaxed. So if the Worry Monster tricks us into feeling scared, we can trick ourselves right back into feeling relaxed. Ha! Take that, Worry Monster!

It is important to practice breathing in calm times to be ready to use this powerful fighting strategy when the Worry Monster is messing with us. Make sure you don't breathe out more air than you breathe in because that alone can activate the anxiety response. People in the midst of a potentially anxiety-producing situation sometimes focus so much on breathing that they forget to exhale or breathe out and then hyperventilate. That's when you breathe in more oxygen than is needed by your body.[19] You can feel sick from too much breathing in. The key is to breathe in slowly and breathe out slowly.

In order to practice slow and calm breathing, I highly recommend starting a regular schedule of breathing. Get your family to do it, too. All you need is one minute in the morning and one minute in the evening. Some families like to spend 5-15 minutes as they experience the positive effects of this simple practice of breathing and mindfulness. There is great benefit to quieting our minds and bodies and allowing room to breathe and just be. Like everything else, it just takes practice.

Things to Remember

- ✔ All worry exists in the future.

- ✔ Stay focused on the present moment.

- ✔ We don't have to believe our thoughts—let them pass.

- ✔ Deep breathing tricks our brain into thinking we are calm.

Things to Do

- ✔ Practice focusing on the present moment. Only think about what is happening right now.

- ✔ Practice letting worrisome thoughts pass. Don't fight them; just notice them and say, "Hmm, it's interesting that I am thinking that thought."

- ✔ Practice deep belly breathing for one minute initially; then increase the time as you start to feel comfortable with it.

CHAPTER 8

Behavioral Interventions: Practice, Practice, Practice!

Act the way that you want to feel.
~ Gretchen Rubin

Now it's time to talk about the behavioral part of cognitive behavior therapy, often referred to as CBT.[20] Behavioral strategies work well with the thinking strategies we discussed in the last two chapters. The wonderful thing about behavior strategies is that they involve *doing* and *practice.* Athletes, students, and musicians all use practice to build skills. You may practice on the balance beam, practice free throws, practice tennis and golf, practice spelling, practice driving, practice guitar, and more. Why do we practice? We practice to get better at something. So how about practicing doing the things that we're afraid of? Practice is the key to working through our fears. It is essential to practice behaviors that allow us to let go of the fears that are holding us back, keeping us from feeling good, taking chances, and meeting our potential.

This chapter lists several behavioral strategies you can use to fight the Worry Monster. You don't need to use all of them. In fact, even if you try one strategy, you will be taking a stand against the

Worry Monster. As you read about these, think about which ones you may want to try.

Systematic Desensitization, Success Ladders, and Baby Steps

Systematic desensitization is the fancy name for what some people call "baby steps" or a "success ladder."[21] This strategy involves breaking down an ultimate goal (let's say the goal is to go swimming) into small steps from the least scary (looking at a picture of a pool or at a real pool from a distance) to the most scary (putting your head under water). The key piece of this strategy is that you slowly step forward, one behavior at a time, until you are familiar, and even bored, with the behavior that once caused you fear, until you reach your ultimate goal (you can go swimming without being afraid). This technique is also called *exposure* because you are exposing yourself to the thing you fear. It isn't much different than learning how to do math. First you learn to count, then add, subtract, multiply, and divide. When you learn to play tennis, first you learn to hit the ball any way you can. Then you learn how to hit a forehand, backhand, volley, and eventually how to serve. All of these things are learned step by step.

I would like to share a story about my daughter and how she faced her fear when she was in kindergarten and first grade. She had challenges at that age with separating from her mother and me and being in new situations by herself. It also took a long time for her to feel that a new situation wasn't new anymore—that is, the third month of school still felt like the first week of school to her, with a new teacher and a new classroom. Dropping her off at preschool was always a challenge because she wanted her mom or me to walk with her to the classroom, and while kindergarten was a bit easier than preschool, she still refused to walk into her kindergarten classroom by herself. She was very anxious about people looking at her, about who was going to be at the school drop-off, and about who knows what other scary things might happen. She absolutely refused to walk by herself from the parent drop-off zone into her school, and there was nothing we could say that would convince her. The school staff person who managed the car drop-off zone tried to bribe her with ice cream every day, but even though she loved ice cream, she still wouldn't leave the safety of the car and walk into her classroom by herself.

Realizing that most kids walk into school on their own in first grade, my wife and I started to practice with our daughter on walking into her class by herself during the second semester of her kindergarten year. At first I would walk her into her kindergarten classroom and follow her to her seat. Then, very slowly and over time, I would walk her only as far as the door and let her find her own seat. I would say, "How about I stand here?" "No! You have to come with me!" she would say. It was definitely a process, but we persisted.

Eventually, I would walk her only as far as her kindergarten cubby, which was just outside of her classroom door and enclosed in the fenced-in kindergarten area. Once she got used to that, I would walk her to the gate of the outside kindergarten area and let her walk to her cubby by herself. From there, we practiced walking to the corner of the building outside the kindergarten area, and that is far as we got by the end of kindergarten. It was not easy, as she really wanted me to walk with her all the way into her classroom most days.

Over the summer, my wife and I talked with her regularly about how one day soon I would drop her off in front of the school, and she would walk through the main school doors and into her first-grade classroom by herself. She was very fearful of doing this and continued to tell us, "No! I don't want to." At the end of summer, we went to the school site and practiced driving in the parking circle together a few times and then having her get out of the car and walk to the main entrance by herself. She could do this during the summer while the school was quiet and no one could see her, but would she do it when school actually started?

The first week of first grade, new first graders were given a week to get adjusted, so we carpooled to school taking other children. We drove her friend and then her cousin to school so that she could practice walking with one of them from the car into their classrooms. She did it! She got out of the car and walked into school, very fast and without me!

Finally, it was time—the deadline had arrived. It was the first day that first graders were supposed to walk into the school entirely by themselves. Just my luck, her cousin and friend wanted to be dropped off by their parents. So it was just her and me and the scary walk into school by herself. I talked with her during the drive to school about how she was "ready to do it," that it was "a piece of cake," and that I was proud of her for all of the practicing that she had done before the first day of school. We pulled in, drove around the corner, and there were all kinds of cars in front of and behind us, as well as a serious-looking person wearing an orange vest trying to keep things moving along.

My daughter was in her carseat looking around. "Things are looking good," I thought to myself. As we approached, I looked in the rearview mirror and saw her eyes get big, and she had a look on her face that said, "There is no way I am getting out of the car and walking into that school!" I said, "Look, we've been practicing; you can do this," and she said, "No, I'm not getting out. I'm not getting out. I'm not getting out!" Now even I was anxious, as the car line was moving and I was expected to keep it moving, yet I had a very stubborn and frightened little girl in my car who wouldn't get out. So like any good father of an anxious child, I said, "If you don't get out, I'm going to get in trouble with the principal!" It happened so fast that I wasn't exactly sure what I had said. To my surprise, she responded, "Fine!" And I'll never forget this: she grabbed her backpack, ripped off her seatbelt, opened the door, and walked into school by herself while I sat in the car sweating and panting.

When her mom picked her up after school, she said that our daughter walked out of school that day with a great big smile on her face (not something she wore often at school). She even called several family members later that day to tell them what she had done.

I tell you this story because it is both about taking baby steps toward an ultimate goal and because it illustrates the importance of overcoming our worries and fears in order to feel more confident and better about ourselves.

Fast-forward four years—because this is also a story about how overcoming anxiety, one victory at a time over the Worry Monster, gradually adds up to changing your brain and your thinking in a more permanent way. When our daughter was a fifth grader, she had the nerve to make fun of her little first-grade sister for not wanting to walk into school on her own. She had totally forgotten how hard it had been for her to get out and walk in by herself at that same age. She actually said, "I can't even imagine why that would be scary." As I have found with many warriors, once a person gets over a fear or worry, she doesn't understand why she was afraid in the first place because the Worry Monster no longer has a hold on her.

Here's another example of using one step at a time, also called a success ladder, to overcome fear. Marcus is 10 and is very afraid of dogs. This fear has slowly but steadily grown and is affecting him and his family regularly. Marcus loves soccer, but he is afraid to go soccer practice and soccer games because there might be a dog there. His parents have gone through all of the cognitive techniques, reasoning with him, but his fear response comes so quickly that he doesn't have time to talk himself through his fears. His response when he sees a dog is to escape and hide, and fast! Together, we developed the following success ladder to help him gradually expose himself to dogs with the ultimate goal of no longer being afraid of them.

The ladder starts with the easiest step at the bottom and works up through harder and harder steps. Marcus designed this ladder with the help of his parents and myself.

The idea is that Marcus will start with the easiest step, the one at the bottom, and work his way up the ladder.

10+	Go to a public place with dogs that are allowed to play off leash.
10	Go to another friend's house with dogs.
9	Go to a friend's house with dogs roaming around.
8	Get close to a dog that is off leash.
7	Be far away from a dog that is off leash.
6	Pet a dog of choice that is on a leash.
5	See dogs more closely at an animal rescue or a dog park.
4	See dogs at a distance at an animal rescue or a dog park.
3	Be at a friend's house with a dog off leash outside or in another room.
2	Watch someone walking a dog on a leash.
1	Look at a book about dogs.

You will notice that there are numbers next to the rungs on Marcus's ladder. These are what I call "scare ratings," which basically means how badly each behavior makes you feel. When making a success ladder, it is important to rate each worry or fear so you know where your starting point is (least scary) and what your ultimate goal is (most scary) using the following scale:[22]

✔ *1-3 Mild Discomfort*: Uncomfortable and nervous, jittery stomach, mild concern, palms are sweaty, knees feel weak

✔ *4-7 Moderate Discomfort*: Scared and anxious, more concern, dry mouth, wanting to leave or escape, feeling tense, trouble swallowing

✔ *8-10 Severe Discomfort*: Very scared and anxious (panic), headache, feeling trapped, dizzy, nauseous, numb, feeling like losing control

On Marcus's success ladder, he felt little distress when holding a book about dogs but was very afraid of being with dogs in an open public place. Being the conscientious person that he is, Marcus took his homework very seriously and practiced each rung, mounting victory after victory over the Worry Monster. I am happy to report that approximately one month after making his ladder, Marcus was able to participate in his soccer games without worry and fear, and he was able to go to parks where there were dogs off leash (and with a big smile on his face, too).

I have another story that is powerful for all people who suffer from fear, and especially for folks who are afraid of insects. It is another example of someone using baby steps to overcome a fear. I saw a video several years that followed a woman through her journey to get over a fear. First the video shows that the woman is so fearful of spiders that she almost faints when looking at a picture of a spider in a book from 15 feet or so away. Through systematic desensitization, baby steps, practicing breathing and relaxation, and getting used to the picture, she is able to take a step closer to the book, and then another step closer. She slowly is able to get closer to the picture, eventually to touch the picture, and then even to read the book. Then she does the same thing with a spider in a box, starting at the end of the room and moving closer and closer until she is sitting near the spider in the box, and then even holding the box. Finally, she does the same thing with a spider out of the box. Again she gets closer and closer, almost fainting from fear at times. At the end of the video she is holding a spider and laughing as the spider walks around on her hand. She did this for five hours over two days and was finally over her fear!

This is a true story. By using a success ladder and practicing each exposure over and over until it isn't scary anymore, you can do amazing things like this woman did. It takes a ton of courage, but you have that courage in you.

Behavioral Rehearsal

This is similar to baby steps in that "rehearsing" is doing the same feared thing over and over and over and over until it gets boring. You can't be bored and anxious at the same time, so anything that you worry about can be done over and over and over again until you are bored with it and it no longer causes problems for you because it doesn't bring up anxious feelings anymore.

Like most of the strategies in this book, this is a simple task, yet it takes a lot of courage to do. If you are afraid of heights or elevators, you practice going up and down elevators until it is boring. Remember, you can start by going up one floor. If you're afraid of bridges, you go over bridges, over bridges, over bridges, and over more bridges until you no longer experience anxiety or fear when you go over them.

I have another story about my daughter. She had a lot of social anxiety and wouldn't look at people when they talked to her; she also wouldn't respond. She would freeze and stare off into the distance. She wouldn't do this with family and close family friends, but she would with everyone else. So what do you do if your dad is a psychologist who can't stand the Worry Monster? You start practicing. First we practiced waving at people on our street when we drove by. Then we practiced saying hello to people on our street when we drove by with the window down. Before I knew it, she was practicing on her own, even when we weren't having a practice session. We then walked around our neighborhood and practiced saying hello to neighbors as we walked by them. It wasn't long before she was excited to answer our door (once she knew it wasn't a stranger) and say hi to whomever was on the other side. Just like walking her into school until she could do it on her own, I could see her confidence rise.

Fast-forward about two years to when she was a third grader and was invited to spend a day in her aunt's third-grade classroom. When the day was over, the other teachers told the aunt that they were impressed with how my daughter had looked them all in the eye, shook their hand, and said, "Nice to meet you." We were blown away. How did that happen? Practice, practice, practice! If you do the feared thing over and over, the fear will eventually go away. So pick a fear to work on, and start practicing!

When I first started piano lessons, I didn't know how to read music, so I tried to memorize everything so no one would know. After a while that got harder to do. At home when I was practicing, I would get frustrated and start to cry. Sometimes I would even get up from the piano and walk away. I thought I would get it eventually, but I didn't. I was so afraid that my teacher would be angry and disappointed in me. My mom finally made me tell my teacher that I couldn't read music. I was very worried, but she wasn't mad! We kept practicing, and suddenly, snap! I got it! I still can't read all of the notes, but I am getting better, and I'm not scared of not knowing anymore.

~ nine-year-old warrior

Response Inhibition (Don't Do It!)

Response inhibition is used primarily for helping people who struggle with OCD (Obsessive-Compulsive Disorder). Remember that a core feature of OCD is doing a compulsive or repetitive behavior (like turning the light switch off and on repeatedly) in order to get rid of the tension and anxiety around a repetitive, irrational, and anxious thought (such as worrying that something bad might happen to you or your parents). People with OCD and/or OCD traits know that the thoughts the Worry Monster is telling them aren't reasonable and are probably never going to happen, yet they are still not willing to take the chance. Further, the anxiety and tension are so uncomfortable that there is a very strong need to make those feelings go away by doing the behavior.

The problem is that if we do the compulsive behavior, it reinforces and supports the idea that the irrational thought is something to be feared and obeyed and that the compulsive behavior is the only thing that can make the feared thought and bad feelings go away. So the response inhibition technique is exactly what it sounds like: the goal is for you to inhibit (or stop) your response (or behavior) to what the Worry Monster (this time the OCD Monster) is telling you.

Examples of behaviors to inhibit include resisting or reducing hand-washing, resisting touching things a certain number of times, resisting repeating what somebody says, resisting walking a certain way down the hall, resisting washing in the shower in a precise order, and so on. Using a timer is an effective way to help increase the response inhibition. The goal with the timer is to see how long you can keep from doing the behavior that you feel like you want to do. Set it for three minutes at first, and see how you feel at the end of that time. If you think you can keep going, set the timer again, this time for five minutes. When you start doing well at this, you can move up to 10 minutes, then even longer. It helps to find something else to do to occupy your mind while you're waiting for the time to pass. You may want to keep a chart of how long you can go without doing the behavior so that you can see how you are improving. Before long, you will see that *you* have control over how long you can hold off doing the behavior. This allows you to have some power over your behavior and helps you realize that you can withstand the uncomfortable feelings. Further, it allows you to see that the irrational thought the OCD Monster is telling you is not true because the scary thing the monster tells you will happen if you don't do the behavior doesn't actually happen.

Another way to battle the OCD Monster is to stop yourself from doing something so many times if you feel like you need to repeat a behavior to feel okay. For example, maybe you feel like you have to touch the doorway on both sides five times each before you can go into your room. But instead of doing that, you decide to touch the doorway only four times. And when that becomes easy, you decide to touch the doorway only three times. Eventually, you will decide that you don't need to do it at all, and then you'll know you've conquered that monster! You can keep a chart to track this kind of progress, too. Just write down how many times you did the behavior each day, and you'll be able to see that you're the one who's in control of what you do—not the monsters!

Fake It to Make It

This is another good strategy for managing our brain and tricking the Worry Monster. The goal of "fake it to make it" is to pretend to be an actor and act like you're not scared. Faking a behavior changes our brain patterns, and it also changes our feelings. For example, research has shown that planned smiling and laughing changes our mood in a positive way.[23] Remember how we talked about how you can't be worried about something and bored with it at the same time? Well, you can't be really upset and scared while you are smiling. This is an easy way to trick the Worry Monster and at the same time have more fun and be less worried and scared.

> *No matter how much Will studied, he worried that he was not prepared for his test and was going to do poorly. I challenged him to pretend that he was prepared and to tell himself over and over, "I am prepared; I am always prepared." Will was convinced it wouldn't work; however, he agreed to try. He was pleased to find out that it helped him to feel more confident and to focus on the test.*
>
> ~ mother of a warrior

> *Fumiko does not like to be away from her father and me. Although she loves gymnastics, she's afraid to go the class. So I promised her that we would get a frozen yogurt if she could trick her instructor by walking in with a smile, saying hi to him, and walking onto the mat (unlike every other day). We laughed at how funny it would be to see her teacher shocked at her behavior. I know she'll still be nervous, but Fumiko is willing to try it.*
>
> ~ mother of a warrior

I once had a client who became nervous in many situations, and finally he became frustrated with feeling that way. He decided that he was going to" act like a winner." When in social situations, he would ask himself, "What would a winner do?" He was surprised at how he was able to feel and act confident when he simply pretended to be a winner. Over time, he admitted that he found himself acting like a winner without giving it much thought. It helps to visualize yourself being a winner before you go somewhere stressful. If you can see yourself pretending to be the person you want to be, you will be well-prepared to give an award-winning performance. Here's another way of saying this that you can remember. You may even want to write it down and keep it with you so you can read it when you start to feel worried or scared:

Act the way you want to feel.

Faking it may seem artificial, especially at first. I have had kids tell me, "But it's not really me. I'm just pretending." That's is a good point. So I tell them that I understand what they are saying, but we are just going to keep trying the behavior as an experiment to see what happens. The thing is, after doing it for awhile, they begin to act out the new behaviors without thinking about them anymore; in other words, the behaviors stop being fake and start being real to them, and they forget that they questioned doing them in the first place.

Pleasure Predicting

Pleasure predicting is similar to "fake it to make it." Many people have anticipatory anxiety, meaning they get really worked up over something that has yet to occur, like a party, performance, or dance, but then once they are at the actual event, they are fine. Sound familiar? Do you ever find it hard to go to new situations or meet new people? Ever wonder why? Well, I think we can guess why now. It's because the Worry Monster is telling you something that is making you nervous. He's telling you about all of the things that *could* go wrong and that he convinces you *will* go wrong.

Pleasure predicting can help you learn more about yourself and find a way to fight the Worry Monster. To use this strategy, ask yourself, "On a scale of 1 to 10, how awful is it going to be when I'm there? 10 is great, and 1 is awful." Many people will give a rating of 1, 2, or 3, meaning it's going to be pretty scary and uncomfortable. But this strategy is like an experiment; you need to find out if your prediction was right, and there's only one way to do that: you go to the party, or the dance, or whatever it is, and you see how bad it actually is. My experience is that it often is not as bad as we think it's going to be. After the event is over, you ask yourself, "So how was it?" If you are honest with yourself, you are likely to rate the event a little higher than you predicted. Maybe it was actually a 5 or a 7. That means it wasn't as bad as you thought. And what does *that* mean? It means the Worry Monster is trying to make you think that things are going to be worse than they ultimately are.

If you try this experiment a few more times, you are likely to find that you tend to feel nervous before an event but that things almost always turn out to be better than you think they'll be. You can then learn to say to yourself, "I know I get nervous before new events, and I feel like I don't want to go, but I also know that I usually end up having more fun than I expect." Remember, the Worry Monster hates it when we talk back to him and challenge him. It is important to notice all of the good or neutral (neither good or bad) things that happened because people who worry tend to only remember the one thing that made them nervous. (Remember the thinking errors from Chapter 5, like filtering and selective attention?)

> *I moved to a new school and was scared to buy lunch. I was afraid that I might not like what they were serving. One day one of my new friends said, "The lunch today is really good." And I just decided, that's it. I am going to do it. And I did—and it really was good! Now I am not afraid to buy lunch, and I've even tried new foods that I never thought I'd like before.*
>
> ~ nine-year-old warrior

Taking a Risk

Planned risk taking is a great technique for worriers and perfectionists. Perfectionists are really good at only doing things they think they can do well, like only turning in schoolwork that is "perfect." So an anti-perfectionistic strategy is to challenge yourself to take a risk at something that you're not good at, to try something new, or to turn in some work that is just okay but not perfect. You can also give your parents and other family members a challenge to do the same thing. Another fun twist is to have a contest: everyone in the family has to do one scary thing for the week, and the person who has the worst experience, as voted by the family, wins a prize.

My parents and even my teacher kept telling me to just turn in my project—that it was more than fine the way it was. They kept saying that it didn't matter that much for my grade and that it was "good enough." I wasn't happy with it and kept finding things that could be done better. Finally, I was exhausted and sick of working on it, so I just made myself turn it in. It felt good to be done with it. I did fine on it and realized that I wasted a lot of time trying to make it perfect when it just needed to be good.

~ 16-year-old warrior

Prescribing Failure

Prescribing failure is similar to taking a risk, as it challenges perfectionists to do something that is not perfect and to survive it. You may think that *survive* is too dramatic a word, but it's really what perfectionists feel—that they won't be able to survive or go on if something does not come out just right. This type of thinking makes perfectionists feel like there's not much they can do because they're always worried about failing. They can't try anything new because they might fail—after all, who does something perfect the first time they try it? Not very many people! And so people who feel this way find themselves stuck only doing the things they've always done, and even then those things don't usually feel good enough. But think of all of the things there are to do in life that are enjoyable but that we have to practice first to get good at! It can feel really good to write a witty story, to play a musical instrument beautifully, to hit a home run, to build a birdhouse or a model car, to paint a lovely picture, to climb to the top of a mountain…and the list goes on. But almost no one can do any of those things without good old-fashioned practice—trial and error—learning how to get better and better and better with each attempt. For perfectionists who are worried about failing, these activities will always be out of reach.

So how can we modify these perfectionistic thoughts? We can purposely try to do something that's *not* perfect. Examples include challenging yourself to turn in messy or incomplete homework, or turning in an art piece that is not "just right." Another example is to either study very little or not study at all for a quiz. Now you're probably thinking, "What are you talking about? I can't do that! What if I get a bad grade?" So what if you do? One bad grade on one homework assignment or one quiz isn't going to ruin your grade for the class. The goal is to be okay with a less-than-perfect performance so you can realize that the sky is not going to fall if you don't do you very best (or beyond your very best) every single time. This is a way to show the Worry Monster that what he is telling you about needing to be perfect is just not true! The world is not going to end, and you are not going to be a bad person if you do something that isn't perfect.

> *I am quite the perfectionist and want everything to be perfect. Thursday nights are the worst for me. People say that once you get past Wednesday, the week gets easier. Nope, not true. Thursday nights are my meltdown nights. Thursday nights are the nights during which I somehow manage to conjure up every possible thing that I could need to worry about; the most trivial thing becomes magnified so it is of just as much importance as the biggest thing. I'm typically told just to go to bed and everything thing will be better in the morning, and it always is. My mom tells me that she actually wants me to fail, as in get an F on something. She's not a bad mom; she just wants me to have that experience of not getting everything perfect or close to perfect.*
>
> ~ 15-year-old warrior

I had a client recently whose school came up with a wonderful activity to help their students take risks and embrace failure. They went on a fieldtrip to a local mall, where the assignment was to get rejected for employment from 10 different stores. My 15-year-old client, who had significant anxiety, came into an appointment with me beaming and stating that he had won the grand prize. His confidence grew so much with each rejection (because he was supposed to get rejected) that he decided to apply to be a manager at a Victoria's Secret store. He laughed as he described the faces of the people who worked there and the customers who were in line. He said, "I never knew how fun it could be to be rejected!"

Some examples of other ways to challenge yourself to be imperfect include asking friends over to play when you know they're going to be busy, trying to be last in a contest at school, or purposely spilling milk on your clothes at lunch. It can actually be fun to think about the funniest ways to make mistakes or fail. You can even ask your parents to try something imperfect at work or in public, too.

More Strategies to Defeat the Perfectionist Monster

Sometimes (okay, maybe not just sometimes) I will see that someone is a better dancer, writer, etc. than me, and I'll want to give up. Sometimes I avoid seeing that imperfection/inferiority in myself by not letting myself be second best, pushing myself to be the best at everything. I can accept that I'm not the best at something if it is something that is new to me, but if I know I can do it and know I am good at it, it is hard to swallow the fact that I am not the best.

~ 14-year-old warrior

Sticking to the Plan

As you may have experienced, procrastination, or putting off doing or finishing something, is a frequent problem among perfectionists. Perfectionists often feel intimidated by even simple projects because they are worried about how hard it will be to make them perfect.

An effective anti-procrastination technique is to choose a topic or activity of focus, make a plan to accomplish the task, and then actually stick to the plan. This is not as easy as it sounds, since perfectionists often find new or "better" ways to do something or feel that they need to learn or do more than the task requires. I once had a client who turned every writing assignment into a giant research paper. Needless to say, by making every writing project larger and longer, this very bright person wasn't able to keep up with her work and fell farther and farther behind. And how do you think she felt to be trying so hard and yet not being able to keep up? Not very good!

There is an old saying: *The perfect is the enemy of the good.* This means that when we try too hard for perfection, we often end up not performing or not turning in something that is good or "good enough"—which is usually all we need to do.

> *Sometimes when people tell me "Good job!" I only half believe them because in the back of my mind, I'm thinking about all of the other things that I could have done and all of the little mistakes I made.*
>
> ~ 15-year-old warrior

I know a nine-year-old who loves to play Minecraft, so he decided to make his own server that his friends could play on. He told his friends that it would be ready in a week, but three weeks later he was still working on it to make it exactly how he envisioned it should be, with no end in sight. We decided to make a plan that he would work on it for two hours a day for the next three days and then invite his friends to play, even if he didn't feel that it was done. This smart kid ended up finding out that not only did his friends like it, but that he could make changes to it whenever he wanted to.

Setting Realistic Expectations

Setting realistic expectations can also be helpful for combating perfectionism.[24] Before you start a task, or sign up to be in a play, or join a team, think about what expectations you have for yourself. Ask yourself if your expectations are reasonable or too narrow, with little room for anything but being the best. Remind yourself that you don't have to do everything right the first time. Try to come up with "good enough" expectations that you can shoot for. Do you want the lead role in the play? Can you be happy with a supporting

role and try another time for the bigger role? Do you want the solo in the concert? Could you be satisfied with a duet instead? Do you want to be the quarterback on the football team? Would just making first string be a good achievement for this year? You may want to write down your "good enough" expectations so that you can remind yourself of them later if you need to.

Sometimes it helps to write down the guidelines for an assignment, activity, or event. This makes the goal concrete. And it can be simple, such as writing down the actual instructions for a school assignment—for example: "Write two sentences for each question," when you usually write a page for each.

> *A lot of the time I'm worried when I get time reminders during in-class writings and tests because I'm not sure that I will have enough time to write down everything I want to say.*
>
> ~ 15-year-old warrior

It can feel really good to participate in a sports team or activity with the goal of just having fun. Perfectionists are so focused on being the best that fun often does not come into the picture. It is a gift for perfectionists to participate in something and not have to worry about how well they do. Maybe your written goal will be this: "Do NOT win the race." This gives you permission to not be the best and yet to realize that the world still turns, the sun still comes up, your friends still like you, and your parents still love you. The Worry Monster (or his good friend the Perfectionist Monster) often tells you that bad things will happen if you aren't always trying so hard to be perfect and to win everything. He is lying, but he is very convincing, as we well know.

Planning Alternative Paths

Planning positive alternative paths is another useful strategy for perfectionist thinkers. Most perfectionists believe that there is only one way to do something: the best! This is usually not because they think they're better than everyone else; it is because they feel that they have failed if they produce anything less than that. It is important to try to develop more flexible and less rigid thinking. Work on creating a mindset that is open to more than one solution to a problem. Try to come up with several possibilities for a problem or project. I know this is hard, but try to tolerate and eventually embrace uncertainty. Remember that it's okay to make mistakes. The Worry Monster hates it when his strategies for making us worried and scared don't work. When he tells you that things aren't going to work out the way you thought, tell him, "So what?"

> *Devin, age 12, always comes up with complex ideas for her projects. If the assignment is to write a paper about an influential person, Devin writes about three people who changed history. If the assignment is to sketch a nature scene, Devin sketches and then paints it in watercolor. While the product is often impressive, the process is grueling for her, and also for her parents. Devin is very hard on herself, often feeling that her work is not good enough. She comes into her parents' room regularly late at night crying and upset, saying she can't do it, and they don't understand her.*
>
> *Devin's parents have decided that they need to help their daughter come up with a plan for her next project—a five-page research paper on an almost extinct species. So they begin by asking her what she is going to research and help her determine the amount of time she needs to complete the project. They then agree on bedtime (since she often stays up late) and what she is willing to turn in if she runs out of time. They also tell her what they are willing to support (answering questions and sitting with her up until 9:00 in the evenings) and what they are not willing to support (late-night meltdowns). They tell her that their goal for her is to turn in a project on time that is "good enough." They know that there will be challenges along the way, but they are committed to helping her develop coping skills.*

Does Devin sound familiar to you? Her story is very common. Late-night meltdowns and accusations to parents who "don't

understand" are unfortunate facts of life in many homes of perfectionistic students. Perfectionists need practice realizing that there are many ways to do something, not just one. Predict the expected challenges that the Worry Monster will give you, and try to remain flexible in your thinking. Remember, while the Worry Monster is sneaky, he is also predictable.

Being Resilient

I have good news for you. Not only are you learning to fight the Worry Monster, you also are learning skills to be a resilient person. Being resilient means being able to handle problems that come your way, cope with them, and find solutions to them. Leading resiliency researchers have identified four main resiliency skills:[25]

✔ *ABCs*: In order to respond to adversity (the "A"), people must recognize their beliefs (the "B") in their thoughts and then engage in challenging those thoughts (the "C"). In this way, they can learn the connection between their thoughts, feelings, and behaviors. You can learn to ask yourself questions about what you are thinking and how you can think differently.

✔ *Challenge Beliefs*: Learn to notice your thinking style and come up with alternatives. Look for evidence to determine whether your thinking is accurate.

✔ *Putting It in Perspective*: Practice preparing for a challenging situation in the future. Think of worst-case beliefs and then healthier, more realistic counter-beliefs, and then make a plan for dealing with the situation.

✔ *Real-Time Resilience*: Have a plan that consists of the other three skills to manage problems when they arise.

So there you have it. By learning how to tame the Worry Monster—understanding how your survival response works, learning that your thoughts determine your feelings and behaviors, understanding that changing your thinking changes your feelings, and learning that practicing doing scary behaviors makes you stronger—you have the necessary skills to take on all of life's challenges!

Things to Remember

✔ Changing our behavior changes our thoughts and feelings.

✔ Worries and fears can be broken into baby steps.

✔ Doing one small feared or worrisome behavior is an important step against the Worry Monster.

✔ Practicing the feared behavior over and over makes the Worry Monster go away.

✔ Not doing what the Worry Monster (or OCD Monster) tells you to do makes the monster weaker.

✔ Pretending to not be scared helps a person do a scary thing (and maybe even enjoy doing it).

✔ It is a victory when a perfectionist can be okay with "good enough" work and effort.

✔ Learning these skills is learning to be resilient and preparing yourself for life.

CHAPTER 9

Patrick, Savannah, and Drew

*Don't believe everything you think. Thoughts are just
that—thoughts.*

~ Allan Lokos

I would like to introduce you to Patrick, Savannah, and Drew, three
courageous young people I know. Like you and me, they know the
Worry Monster and his friends well. They have graciously given me
permission to use their stories so that others can learn to fight the
Worry Monster as they have. Through their experiences, you will
see how understanding the fear response in their bodies, becoming
aware of the Worry Monster and his tricks and tactics, and devel-
oping thinking and behavior plans helped them regain control of
their lives and drive the Worry Monster away. (Their names have
been changed to protect their privacy.)

Patrick

Patrick is a 10-year-old fifth grader who gets pretty good
grades but who worries about some of the things that are happening at his home. His father might have to take another job, which
would mean the family selling their home and moving to a different
state. Patrick started to feel anxious about this possibility, and soon
he started doing some things that he hadn't done before to try to

make himself feel better. He began washing his hands several times a day, switching the light switch on and off, touching certain objects and people over and over, tapping himself in a particular way, and jumping in and out of bed several times at night. He said that he did those things "to get rid of the freaky feelings." Patrick also said that he felt angry and scared that something bad would happen if he didn't do those things. In addition, Patrick didn't like change. His worst times were when he had to move on to another task or activity, when there was an unexpected change, or at the thought of something changing.

Helping Patrick Fight the Worry and OCD Monsters

In order to give Patrick the tools he needed to fight the Worry Monster, we had to use several techniques and strategies. The first thing we did was to help Patrick understand the fight or flight response. Next we talked about the Worry Monster and the OCD Monster, and Patrick learned all about how the monsters become tricky and powerful. We then developed strategies to undermine the Worry and OCD Monsters' power, and we put together a team, led by his father and supported by his mother, to conquer the two monsters. Finally, we developed a "toolbox" of strategies that Patrick could carry with him at all times.

What follows are a few examples of how to talk about the Worry and the OCD Monsters. I asked Patrick some simple questions that helped him learn quite a bit about his monsters and gain a sense of control over them. You can ask yourself these questions, or have your parents ask you them so they can help you discover the answers.

Identifying Patrick's Irrational and Worrisome Thoughts

Dan: "What does the OCD Monster say to you?"

Patrick: "The OCD Monster always says something bad is going to happen. He makes me feel that I have to touch things and wash my hands or something bad will happen."

Changing Patrick's Thinking

Dan: "How can you change your thinking? What can you tell the Worry and OCD Monsters so they don't trick you?"

Patrick started to talk back to the monsters. Whenever he would think the scary thoughts, he would respond by saying to himself: "The monster doesn't have magic powers. My team is stronger and more powerful than he is. He's just a bully and a coward."

Patrick's Success Ladder and Scare Steps

Once Patrick learned about the fight or flight response, and about how the Worry and OCD Monsters tell him things to make him worried and scared, and that he could change his thinking to have more rational and less scary thoughts, we created a success ladder for him, with 1 being the easiest step and 10 being the hardest at the top rung of the ladder. The numbers on the left are his scare ratings. You'll notice that Patrick's ladder is not filled with things he must do, but instead it consists mostly of things that he must try *not* to do.

10	Touching something he has been afraid of
9	Resist touching another person
7-8	Resist jumping in and out of bed
5-6	Resist touching various parts of his body
4	Resist washing hands
3	Resist turning light switches on and off
1-2	Resist touching doorways

Response Inhibition (Don't Do It!) and Practice, Practice, Practice!

Patrick started with the least scary behavior on his list, and each week he practiced not doing the behavior the OCD and Worry Monsters told him he had to do. He worked on a behavior until it became a 1 and then moved on to the next rung on the ladder.

Touching doorways and turning light switches on and off quickly became a 1.

Patrick developed a healthier ritual of washing his hands just three times a day instead of six or seven times. Eventually this new habit became a 1.

Patrick continued to work his way up the ladder. Some days were tougher than others, but with the support of his parents, he kept practicing. As he experienced victories over the Worry and OCD Monsters, he became more and more motivated to continue to battle them.

However, Patrick's worry continued. Even though Patrick achieved victory after victory over the OCD Monster, the Worry Monster not only remained, but at times became stronger. Now Patrick started to worry about natural and other disasters happening—tsunamis, plane crashes, tornados, and floods. This kind of thing is common when fighting worry and anxiety, as the Worry Monster is stubborn and does not like to lose his power. Conquering the Worry Monster isn't easy, and sometimes we feel like we're going backwards, but we just have to keep practicing healthy thoughts and behaviors. If we do that, we eventually will beat him. In addition to continuing to challenge and change Patrick's thinking, we developed more strategies for fighting the Worry Monster.

Strategies for Combating Worry

- ✔ *Schedule worry time*: Patrick decided that he would set aside 15 minutes in the evening to worry. So when he was worrying during the day, he would tell himself, "I will save this for my worry time later tonight." He found that this helped distract him from his worry throughout the day, and he often forgot what his worry had been about when night came.

- ✔ *Make a worry box*: Patrick decided to make and decorate his very own worry box. He would write down his worries in the morning and at night (when he could remember them) and place them in his worry box for safe-keeping. That meant that he didn't have to remember the worries because they were in the box, and he could let the worries stay in the box until he was ready to look at them again.

Coping Plan: Toolbox

We developed a "toolbox" that Patrick could take with him wherever he went, and he could use it whenever the OCD or Worry Monster came for a visit. While Patrick kept his toolbox in his head, some kids like to keep theirs on a small notepad or a note card they carry with them in their pocket or backpack. With these tools, Patrick felt more prepared and equipped to fight the monsters whenever they showed up. His toolbox consisted of these strategies:

- ✔ Breathe calmly.

- ✔ Visualize a calming place.

- ✔ Know what it is that makes you first start to worry.

- ✔ Identify your thoughts: *How are my thoughts making me worry?*

- ✔ Challenge the thoughts, change the thoughts, and talk back to the Worry Monster and the OCD Monster.

- ✔ Motivate yourself to face the fear, and give yourself a reward.

- ✔ Remind yourself that anxious feelings *always* go away eventually.

- ✔ Practice doing the positive behaviors over and over.

- ✔ *Refuse* to let worry run your life!

Patrick's Success Ladder After Scaring Away the Worry Monster

Was Patrick successful? I think so. Here is how he now rates these behaviors:

- ✔ Not touching doorways: 0
- ✔ Not turning light switches on and off: 0
- ✔ Not washing hands: 3
- ✔ Not touching himself: 0

✔ Not jumping in and out of bed: 0
✔ Not touching someone: 0
✔ Touching something scary: 0

Patrick's Current Thinking

✔ "The OCD Monster uses stories that are made up, just like in my books."

✔ "Science calms me. I am going to learn more about natural disasters."

✔ "I don't let the OCD Monster bully me like I used to."

✔ "I just tell myself that he can't do the things he says he will do."

✔ "When I live with it, it goes away; when I fight it, it makes me do it over and over again."

Patrick's Worry and OCD Monsters come back to visit from time to time, particularly when there is a new, big change like a move or a new school. However, Patrick knows his monsters well and uses his toolbox to deal with them. His parents remind him of how to challenge his thinking and about all of the successes he's had. As a result, the OCD and Worry Monsters do not hang around much anymore, and they certainly are less powerful than they used to be.

Savannah

Savannah is an 11-year-old sixth grader. She is a bright child who has a history of stomach problems (she is lactose-intolerant), which have required her to take medication. She is very aware of how she feels—"perhaps too much," her parents note—as she is constantly assessing how her stomach feels. In the middle of the fifth grade, Savannah had a 24-hour stomach virus that caused her to have stomach problems which took three months to recover from. She vomited three times over a few hours on day one of the virus. Within the first week following the virus, she was scared to eat. For several weeks after that, her fear increased.

Shortly after her vomiting episode, Savannah stopped eating and drinking regularly. She was so afraid of vomiting that she stopped eating breakfast "so I won't have an upset stomach and throw up at school." It wasn't long before Savannah stopped eating lunch as well. She was also fearful that her parents wouldn't be there to help her if she did get sick, saying, "What if throw up? How will you help me? What if I can't get a hold of you?" Already very thin, Savannah was losing weight from not eating. She began to become scared and angry before school and soon refused to go.

Helping Savannah Fight the Worry Monster

As with Patrick, Savannah and her parents needed to use several strategies to help her fight her Worry Monster. As you can guess, Savannah first had to understand how the Worry Monster was responsible for how she was feeling. She learned about the amygdala, the role of adrenaline and how it made her body feel, the fight or flight response, and how she needed to use her thinking brain to overpower her emotional brain.

Savannah's parents were very involved in helping her "out-think" the Worry Monster. They talked to Savannah about how the Worry Monster was making her body feel. They became quite skilled at talking to their daughter about what the Worry Monster was doing to her. Through this kind of questioning, it became apparent that the Worry Monster was telling Savannah two very simple but scary things.

Identifying Savannah's Worrisome Thinking

Dan: "What is the Worry Monster telling you when you feel scared?"

Savannah: "That it might happen again. If I eat, I will throw up again."

Being a bright young girl, Savannah understood that she was smarter than the Worry Monster and that the Worry Monster was just a dumb bully. She practiced changing her worrisome thoughts and also talking back to the Worry Monster.

Challenging and Changing Savannah's Thinking

Dan: "What can you say to the Worry Monster when
              he tells you those lies?"

Savannah: "Just because my stomach feels uncomfort-
              able, that doesn't mean I will vomit. The Worry
              Monster is just a bully who is trying to trick me.
              So what if I throw up?"

Through our conversations, Savannah also learned that all of
the Worry Monster's thinking was based in the future and that if she
focused on the present, she always felt fine. Right away, Savannah
began to achieve victories against the Worry Monster. She still had
her fear of vomiting, but she started eating regularly again. And as
she continued to work her plan, her fear of vomiting faded. She
became less emotional, and happiness returned to her life.

However, as we saw with Patrick, the Worry Monster can be
persistent and can come back for a visit now and then to see if his
strategies still work. Sometimes this happens when something else
stressful is going on in our lives. Other times it occurs as children
get older and their bodies and brains start changing during adolescence. And other times it happens when people forget about the
Worry Monster and stop doing the things that made him go away
in the first place, like realize his words are lies! About six months
after we began working to fight the Worry Monster, he came back
to Savannah with full force, giving her one panic attack and then
another. He had found his way back in.

He once again started to bully Savannah and got her to think:
"My stomach feels weird. I might throw up. Remember how bad
it was last time?"

The Worry Monster made Savannah so scared that she was
afraid to go to school. He convinced her that she would vomit
at school, that she wouldn't be able to handle it, and that her
parents wouldn't be there to help her. Savannah stopped eating
again, and there were daily meltdowns about going to school,
with Savannah often refusing to go. It was clear that the Worry

Monster had a tight grip on this young girl, and she needed her team to help her.

We developed a plan in which we talked to Savannah's teacher and principal about the Worry Monster and how he was telling Savannah that she might vomit, thereby keeping her from going to school. Her principal became Savannah's "go to" person when the Worry Monster was making her scared, and her teacher understood that there might be times when Savannah needed to leave the classroom to talk to the principal without having to answer a lot of questions about it. And her parents needed to fight the Worry Monster for Savannah by insisting that she go to school, even when she didn't feel she could. This was very hard for Savannah's parents because they hated to see her cry, but they knew that the only way to beat the Worry Monster was to make Savannah ignore him by going to school, even when she really, really, really didn't want to.

Reinforcing the Battle Plan

What follows is the plan that everyone agreed to. Savannah wanted this plan to work, but she was still scared, and the Worry Monster wouldn't stop putting doubts in her head.

- ✔ Go to school at all costs!
- ✔ Have the teacher and principal help support her at school.
- ✔ Carry a cell phone for calling her parents if she does get sick.
- ✔ Challenge the Worry Monster's thinking ("So what?").
- ✔ Remember that eating is healthy and that vomiting helps us survive (it gets rid of the bad stuff).
- ✔ Focus on the present—everything is fine right now!
- ✔ Read to distract herself.

With tremendous courage, Savannah returned to school. She used her cell phone to text and call her parents from the principal's office when she was scared. At first, she would miss entire classes. But it wasn't long before she only needed to stay in the office for about 15 minutes before returning to her classroom. Savannah mounted victory after victory against the Worry Monster, eventually not needing to go to the principal's office or to call her parents at all.

Over time, Savannah reported only vaguely thinking about vomiting, but even when she did, it didn't scare her anymore. She still knows that the Worry Monster is always lurking and may not be far away—may even try to come back for a visit. However, she also knows how he messes with her and that it is very important that she not let him convince her that she can't or shouldn't go to school. In addition, Savannah knows that she has a plan and a strong team to support her.

Drew

Now I want to tell you about Drew, who is 12 and in seventh grade. Drew's story shows how elaborate and detailed an understanding one can have regarding the monsters, how they work, and how they can be outsmarted.

Drew is a bright, kind, and conscientious person. He is a strong student and excels in all of the sports he plays. However, when I first met him, he didn't like to step on lines or touch corners. He also tapped door jambs and opened and closed books repetitively. Despite having an A+ in six out of his seven classes, he worried about his school performance and felt that he needed to get the "perfect" grade. Drew sometimes had different numbers in his head that represented certain things to him—for example, 3 was for sports over the weekend, and 5 was the smart number. Drew (encouraged by the OCD Monster) created a system of rules for using the numbers, and he believed that he needed to follow those rules to think "correctly." As an example, he believed that he needed to think about the number 5 when he was opening and closing his backpack. He also felt that he needed to erase a word he was writing if he wasn't thinking correctly as he wrote it or else he feared that he would turn into a bad kid, like others in his class who were poor students and got in trouble.

As you probably have guessed by now, I talked with Drew about the fight or flight response and how our scary or anxious thoughts activate our survival response. I then told him about the Worry Monster and the OCD Monster and how both of those monsters seemed to be ganging up on him to make him worry and do things he didn't want to do. Drew understood these things right away, saying, "It's a pretty tricky monster." He told me that the OCD Monster first came to him when he was in sixth-grade math, when he "needed something to do to reassure myself."

Identifying Drew's Worrisome Thinking

Dan: "What does the Worry Monster tell you?"

Drew: "If I get a lower grade, it might lead to more lower grades. My teacher will look down on my abilities. Other people won't think I'm as smart as they thought at first. I may never be able to get an A+ again."

Changing Drew's Thinking

Dan: "How can you change your thinking? What can you tell the Worry and OCD Monsters so they don't trick you?"

Drew came up with the following new thoughts to combat the Worry Monster: "Not getting an A on an assignment will affect my grade but not my future test scores. My teacher may wonder what happened, but it really doesn't matter to her. Other people aren't going to think any different of me for it. But I most likely will do well anyway because I know how to study."

Setting Up a Behavior Plan

I taught Drew about response inhibition and the importance of *not* doing what the OCD Monster told him to do. He decided that he would start by resisting erasing words when he was writing and also not doing things the number of times the OCD Monster told him to. It was important for Drew to select only one or two things to work on since he was a high achiever and put a lot of pressure on himself to excel.

Drew was able to earn some initial victories over the monsters. He reported that he was able to resist erasing words, that he stopped repeatedly opening and closing books, and that he resisted having to touch things a certain number times. In fact, Drew started getting irritated at the monsters for making him do things he didn't want to do and for making him use so much mental energy. He added some new challenging thinking:

✔ "Why would I want to do that?"
✔ "I'm not going to worry about that!"

As we continued to talk about the Worry and OCD Monsters, Drew started to gain an understanding of how they work together to mess with him. One day we discovered that there was actually a third monster, the Perfectionism Monster, that often joined in as well. Drew explained to me about how these three monsters worked together against him.

> Drew: *The OCD Monster and the Perfectionism Monster team up. The OCD Monster is the muscle, and the Perfectionist Monster is the brains. He comes up with the ideas about being perfect, and the OCD Monster puts them to use.*
>
> Dan: *Where does the Worry Monster come in?*
>
> Drew: *The Worry Monster starts everything off because if you don't worry, you can't be a perfectionist. They all target your weaknesses. I thought it was weird why I did all this stuff, but now I know why.*
>
> Dan: *How do you think you can outsmart them?*
>
> Drew: *I know the three different monsters, and I have to separate them. If you keep the three of them apart, even though they are naturally bonded, you can fight them separately. The OCD Monster is going to make me erase words. The Perfectionist Monster wants me*

> *to stay the same person and tells me that if I don't do what the OCD Monster says, I'm not going to be who I am. The Worry Monster is going to tell me to hurry up and not erase so I won't run out of time. He makes it seem like he is my friend when he is actually a double agent, since he tries to force me to do it but makes me think he is on my side.*

Dan: *You really have these guys figured out. I'll bet you know what you need to say to them to take away their power.*

Drew: *Yes! For the OCD Monster, I can say, "This is outrageous! You can't make me do that!" To the Perfectionist Monster, I can say, "No matter what, I am going to be who I am." Finally, to the Worry Monster, I can say, "We both know you're not trying to help me!"*

Drew's Toolbox

Drew felt that he needed a good list of statements to say to the monsters, as well as strategies to fight them. We came up with the following:

- ✔ "Bring it on!"
- ✔ "So what?"
- ✔ Push the thought away and ignore it.
- ✔ Do the opposite of what the monster says.
- ✔ Remember that I have stood up against them before.

Drew continues to impress me with his strong understanding of the monsters and his courageous stand against them. He continues to chip away at the monsters' power and mount new victories over them.

Chapter Summary

Patrick, Savannah, and Drew were able to fight the Worry Monster (and Perfectionist and OCD Monsters) because they had new information about their brain and body. They were told about the Worry Monster and what he did to make them feel scared and awful. They were able to identify what the Worry Monster told them to make them feel that way and also how they could think new thoughts to change the way they felt, as well as to make the Worry Monster less powerful. They learned strategies for dealing with the worry and fear and developed a set of "tools" they could rely on when the monster came to visit. They also learned that they were not alone in their struggle but that they had a team to fight and ultimately tame the monster.

Things to Remember

- ✔ Patrick, Savannah, and Drew learned how their Worry, OCD, and Perfectionism Monsters worked and then took steps to fight them.

- ✔ They became aware of what the monsters told them and learned to challenge and replace their thoughts with different thoughts.

- ✔ They engaged in behaviors that made them stronger and made the monsters weaker.

- ✔ They developed a plan and had a toolbox of strategies to use against the monsters.

- ✔ They gained confidence as they mounted their victories.

- ✔ They made the monsters weak and powerless.

Things to Do

- ✔ Get ready to make a plan to fight your Worry Monster!

- ✔ You can do this!

CHAPTER 10

Making a Plan to Tame the Worry Monster

When you change the way you look at things, the things you look at change.

~ Wayne Dyer

You are now armed with the knowledge you need to make your battle plan. As you know, when the Worry Monster succeeds in having you avoid the feared thing, situation, or feeling, the avoiding actually reinforces the fear and makes it stronger. Therefore, our goal is to face the Worry Monster, conquer him, and render him powerless! You are going to do this by using your great big thinking brain (frontal cortex) to override your small emotional brain (amygdala). You are going to use the simple thinking techniques of identifying and changing your thinking, as well as engaging in practice sessions to slowly overcome your fears. You are also going to develop a toolbox of strategies that you can use at any time.

Making and Working the Plan

I have broken up everything that we have discussed in this book so far into nine simple steps. You may want to go through each step, or you may find that after doing the first few steps, you can skip a few to focus on the ones that are most important for you. That is fine! Don't let the Worry Monster tell you that you are doing it wrong. By now, you know the key elements of fighting the Worry Monster: remember how our survival (fight or flight) response works, and develop thinking and behavior strategies to outsmart what the Worry Monster tells us. The strategies listed in the previous chapters are meant to be a "menu" of choices. You do not need to use all of them. Try the ones that you think will work, and if they don't work, try others. The most important thing is to make the monster go away!

Step 1: Remember How Your Brain and Body Work When You Are Scared
　　Remember these important points:

- ✔ We have a "fight or flight" survival response that is designed to keep us alive.

- ✔ Our amygdala (fear center) runs our in-body security system that is designed to keep us alive.

- ✔ Adrenaline is sent through our bodies to make us run fast and fight hard.

- ✔ Our body feels a certain way when we are nervous, worried, or scared.

- ✔ Our thoughts are responsible for triggering our amygdala and sending adrenaline through our body.

- ✔ If we change our thinking, our feelings will change, too.

- ✔ If we practice something we are afraid of over and over, we won't be afraid of it anymore.

Step 2: Identify Body Feelings
　　When your amygdala gets activated, you will feel the physical sensations of worry and fear in your body, especially your head, chest, stomach, and throat. Remember, this is the normal body response to fear. As we discussed, these are your indicators that the

Worry Monster is visiting and picking on you. Helpful questions to ask yourself include:

✔ Where do I feel it in my body?

✔ What happens when I feel nervous or scared?

✔ What are my warning signs?

✔ How do I know when I am scared or worried?

It can be hard to answer these questions when you are worried or scared. You may be better able to answer them when you are not scared or when your worry or fear is at a low level. It is okay if this step is hard. Just keep at it.

Step 3: Externalize the Problem

This is the part where you identify your monster and figure out how he works and what he tells you. Remember:

✔ The Worry Monster is a bully who is responsible for making you (and all of us) think worrisome and scary thoughts.

✔ The Worry Monster's job is to keep you from enjoying life. He gets joy from picking on children (and adults) and making them worried and scared.

✔ The Worry Monster is both dumb and smart. He is dumb because he uses the same strategy over and over. He tells people that bad things are going to happen even though he can't really make them happen. (He lies about this all the time.) He is smart because he hides and uses the same tricks over and over, and most people don't realize he's there. (He is very sneaky and can creep up on us.)

✔ Look at the picture of the Worry Monster. See how silly and pathetic he looks. Laugh at him.

✔ Remember the scene in *The Wizard of Oz* when Dorothy and her friends found out who the Wizard really was, and think about how the characters became strong and fearless when

they realized that the Wizard was not powerful and was just tricking them—just like the Worry Monster does to you.

✔ The more you talk about the Worry Monster and gang up on him with your allies, like your parents and maybe even your teachers, the sooner he will go away.

Step 4: Make a Worry List

Making a worry list is more fun than you might think, especially if you do it as a family.[26] But whether this becomes a family activity or something that you do on your own, the goal is for you to make a list of *everything* you worry about. It is a basically a brainstorming session. Remember that the Worry Monster doesn't like us to talk about him or how he works, so the more things you put on the list, the better.

Once you have made the list of worries, it's time to decide how scary each item is. Think about each worry or fear, and give it scare rating of between 1 and 10 using the following scale:

✔ *1-3 Mild Discomfort*: Uncomfortable and nervous
✔ *4-7 Moderate Discomfort*: Scared and anxious
✔ *8-10 Severe Discomfort*: Very scared and anxious (panic)

Once you have done this, put the worries and fears in order starting with the most powerful (severe) at the top and going down to the least powerful (mild). Now you have a list of all of your worries and fears in order of most to least scary. You'll want to start tackling the easier ones at the bottom first so that you can work your way up to the harder ones as you get better and better at telling the Worry Monster that you're not going to listen to him any more!

Step 5: Make a Success Ladder

Making a success ladder is optional at this point. You can either use the ranked worry list that you made, or you can choose a behavior from the worry list and make a success ladder out of it by breaking it down into baby steps, with the ultimate fear or goal at the top of the ladder and the least scary behavior at the bottom.

You will need to decide whether you can start with a single fear like riding an escalator or whether the task needs to be broken into parts so that you can gain confidence by becoming used to each baby step along the way to conquering your fear.

Step 6: Identify Worrisome and Fearful Thinking

This is the part where you think about what the Worry Monster tells you to make you feel worried and scared. I know this sounds repetitive, but it is important to keep talking about this over and over (like practice) until you are comfortable with this way of thinking about your worries and fears.

Take out your worry list, and expose the Worry Monster's secrets by writing down what he tells you to make you feel scared and worried. For example:

Worries	What the Worry Monster Tells Me
Being left alone	I might get left at school. Something bad might happen to my mom.
Sleeping alone	Someone might break into our house. I might have a nightmare.
Taking tests	What if I forget everything? What if I fail?

Get the picture? Just list your worries and then the thoughts that make you worry.

Step 7: Change and Modify Thinking

Now that you have a list of worries that includes the things the Worry Monster tells you, you can see the different types of thinking errors we discussed in Chapter 5. Of course, you can skip this part if you want to get to the next step without identifying your worry thinking patterns.

Take the top one to three worries or fears that you are willing to work on. Remember, you can use rewards to motivate yourself to tackle a fear. You will definitely want to include your parents in this part since they are often important in the reward plan. Examples of rewards include frozen yogurt or extra screen time after accomplishing a victory or even attempting a behavior on your plan.

Go back to the list where you wrote what the Worry Monster tells you, and next to those thoughts, write down new thoughts that are healthier and more realistic. Your list might look like this:

Old Thought (What the Worry Monster Tells Me)	New Thought
I might get left at school.	I have never been left before.
Something bad might happen to my mom.	My mom is strong and can take care of herself.
Someone might break into our house.	We always lock our doors and windows.
I might have a nightmare.	Nightmares are scary, but I am always okay when they are over.
What if I forget everything?	I never forget everything.
What if I fail?	I studied for the test. So what if I fail?

Here are useful questions to ask yourself when you are working on changing your thoughts and when the Worry Monster is visiting:

✔ What am I thinking?

✔ What is the thinking error involved?

✔ Is the thought realistic? Is it true? Do I have evidence to prove that it's true or not true?

✔ How can I think about this differently?

✔ What can I think instead that is more true and realistic?

With time and practice, it will get easier and easier to answer these questions, and each time you answer them, you are pushing the Worry Monster a little bit farther out the door.

Step 8: Practice, Practice, Practice!

This is where the real work comes in. You are going to choose behavioral practice activities to tackle the Worry Monster head on. Remember, you can either work on a fear in its entirety, like walking into school on your own, or accomplish it in steps as part of a success ladder, in which you start by walking part of the way into school by yourself.

They key principle here is to start with something that you think you can handle with very little fear, such as waving to a neighbor while driving in the car. You will want to start with something that isn't too hard so you can have an early victory that will help you gain confidence in your ability to fight the Worry Monster. Once you have some success, do the same victorious behavior a few more times until it becomes easy and boring. The key is for there to be zero feelings of anxiety with each step forward you are taking.

Remember that you can reward yourself for each success you have, even if it's a small one. Rewards can be simple, but they will help you motivate yourself to keep going, and they're a way to celebrate the victories you've had.

One family I know created a "Victory Chart." The chart serves two purposes for them: first, it's where they list their goals, and second, it's also where they record the fears or worries that they have conquered, and it reminds them of all of the negative things they have overcome. The chart hangs below a picture that shows how the amygdala makes us worry. Both the picture and the Victory Chart are posted on the back of their son's bedroom door, and he looks at it often. Other families take a picture of the Worry Monster and put stickers, stars, or pushpins over him every time there is a victory until the Worry Monster is covered and disappears. If you want to do this, you can find a full-color version of Worry Monster at http://bit.ly/KidWarrior or http://bit.ly/TheWorryMonster. The image is available as a pdf file that you can print out and use.

Step 9: Develop a Coping Toolbox

Regardless of whether you conquer the Worry Monster quickly or whether you take baby steps to defeat him, you will benefit from having a personalized toolbox to help you take on the Worry Monster when he shows up. This toolbox usually consists of strategies like deep breathing, understanding where in your body you feel the worry, what makes you start worrying or feeling scared, common things to say to yourself to challenge your thinking, and activities that distract you and help you relax.

When designing your toolbox, ask yourself:

✔ How do I know when the Worry Monster is visiting?

✔ What can I do to combat him?

✔ What thinking strategies should I use?

✔ What distracts me from worry and fear?

✔ What helps me feel more confident and relaxed?

Here is a list of some tools that you can choose from. Feel free to add to this list:

✔ Take deep breaths.

✔ Focus on the present moment.

✔ Use positive self-talk ("I can do this!").

✔ Ask yourself what you are thinking.

✔ Change your thinking.

✔ Talk back to the Worry Monster ("Take a hike, you cowardly bully!").

✔ Ignore the Worry Monster ("So what?").

✔ Distract yourself with another activity.

✔ Exercise.

✔ Seek support from a friend, parent, or teacher.

✔ Use your worry box.

✔ Reserve your worries for worry time later.

You can take your toolbox with you everywhere you go. Nobody will see it, especially the Worry Monster. Knowing that you have these tools will help you feel more confident and be ready for the Worry Monster anytime and anywhere!

And Poof, He's Gone!

There you have it. You have just learned the secret to fighting and taming the Worry Monster. He is no longer a mystery. He is no longer a threat. He is no longer lurking in the shadows. Well, he is still lurking, but no longer in the shadows. You have exposed him. You know all, or at least most, of his tricks and have several strategies to conquer him and render him powerless. Look at him; he's getting so small and puny! Poor Worry Monster. He needs to go away and find someone else to pick on.

Poof!

Things to Remember

✔ Make a plan that you think will work so that you can have a victory.

✔ You don't need to do every step of the plan.

✔ Remember to focus on baby steps and small victories.

✔ Talk about the Worry Monster, and expose his tricks.

✔ Challenge his worrisome thinking, and change it to be more true and real.

✔ Seek help and support. Gang up on him!

✔ Talk back to the Worry Monster, and show him who's boss!

Things to Do

✔ Make a plan.

✔ Work the plan.

✔ Be brave!

✔ Don't give up!

✔ Banish the Worry Monster!

Chapter 11

Troubleshooting and Healthy Habits

The trick is to enjoy life. Don't wish away your days waiting for better ones ahead.

~ Marjorie Hinckley

You will probably experience some immediate positive results with your battle plan. Sometimes you will see surprisingly fast progress, but other times either you may be too scared or the Worry Monster may fight back and make it hard to win a victory against him. This chapter will help you if you get stuck and can't seem to defeat that bully monster.

Troubleshooting

Here is a list of ideas and strategies to consider if you are having trouble working the plan and taking on the Worry Monster.

Start with a Victory

Make sure you are starting small enough on the success ladder. Sometimes we get excited about conquering our fears, and we go too fast. Stay with the small behaviors, and do them over and over until you are ready for another one. You will know when you're ready because the behavior practice will become easy and boring.

Look at Your Reinforcement Plan

Your reward plan may not be strong enough to overpower what the Worry Monster is telling you. Talk with your parents about what you can agree on that would help you take a courageous step against the Worry Monster. You are just trying to get a small victory. Remember, baby steps.

Try Working on a Different Worry or Fear

Sometimes the fear you are working on may be too scary, and you may have more success tackling another one. If that's the case, go back to your worry list, and choose another fear to work on. Again, start with an easy first step so you can win a victory.

Try a Different Thinking Strategy

Sometimes the thinking strategies you come up with simply don't work. Look at the ones you have created (for example, "I don't need to worry about my mom not coming to pick me up because my mom *always* comes to get me") and try a new one (for example, "My mom will be here soon"). Sometimes just saying something in a different way can be helpful.

Distraction

Sometimes we just need to come up with ways to be distracted from our fears. This can be reading, limited screen time, riding a bike, or whatever takes your mind off of the worry and fear. Even though doing this doesn't make you directly face your fear, you are *living* and *doing* things instead of just sitting around and worrying.

Add More Tools

If you are having trouble taking positive steps and engaging in practice sessions, you may need more tools in your toolbox. Be creative, as virtually anything that helps you battle the Worry Monster can go in your toolbox. You may need to practice some deep breathing, carry something that gives you courage in your pocket, or talk to or text your parents or a trusted adult every time the Worry Monster is visiting.

The Worry Monster does not like to be defeated, so he hangs on for as long as he can. The additional strategies in this chapter should help you fight against him and gain some results. Remember, the goal is to know how to handle him when he visits, not to keep him from ever visiting, because everyone worries about something from time to time. You just keep getting better and better at dealing with the Worry Monster when you practice making him go away.

Diet and Exercise

What you eat and drink and how much you exercise and sleep are important things to think about when fighting the Worry Monster. When we do not take care of these health essentials, it opens the door for the Worry Monster to walk in.

With regard to diet, it is important that you eat a steady dose of protein throughout the day. Many kids experience low blood sugar, also known as *hypoglycemia*. Low blood sugar usually occurs a few hours after breakfast, and it looks a lot like what happens when people start to feel anxiety: they feel dizzy, start sweating, feel weak, and their heart beats really fast.[27] It is not uncommon for some children and teens to experience hypoglycemia several times throughout the day and wrongly think that their problem must be anxiety.

If you think you might be experiencing low blood sugar at certain times during the day, you can create a simple test to find out. Make sure you eat protein for breakfast (for example, cereal with milk, an egg, a peanut butter sandwich, some cheese). Then make sure to eat a protein snack mid-morning (cheese stick, peanut butter crackers, yogurt), protein again for lunch, a mid-afternoon protein snack, and protein again at dinner. If you feel a lot better and not as sad, angry, or crabby when you eat this way, then you can be pretty sure you need to eat more protein, including a mid-day protein boost.

The following substances are ones that you should try to stay away from because the effects of using them actually feel just like the effects of adrenaline and can make people feel anxious: caffeine, energy drinks, nicotine, and alcohol.[28] In addition to avoiding those, regular exercise will help in fighting the Worry Monster and keeping him at bay. Exercise burns adrenaline and makes your heart less sensitive to it.[29] If it's not already a part of your daily routine, add daily exercise to your plan. It's not just good for your body, it will help make the Worry Monster powerless. Exercise can include any number of activities that you may enjoy: swimming, shooting baskets, hiking, soccer, dodgeball, tennis, martial arts, jump roping, rock climbing, bicycling, dancing, gymnastics, yoga, and more.

> *After I swim or play tennis, I feel calm. I am a lot happier after I exercise.*
>
> ~ nine-year-old warrior

Sleep

People need sleep in order to think clearly, learn, and manage their feelings and behaviors. It is recommended that five- to 12-year-olds get 10-11 hours per night and teens get a little more than nine hours per night (although some do fine with eight and a half hours).[30] How much sleep to you need?

> *When I am learning something new, I am afraid I will never get it. I get emotional. I hit myself. I say I am a disappointment. Usually I am tired, and once I rest, I am better the next day.*
>
> ~ eight-year-old warrior

The key is to try to get as much sleep as you need, but also not to worry about your sleep too much. The more you worry about not getting enough sleep and what will happen if you don't sleep, the longer you will be awake. To help you sleep better, here are some tips:[31]

- ✔ Plan a consistent time for going to sleep, seven days a week.

- ✔ Reduce light exposure in the hour before sleep, especially TV/cell phone/computer screens.

- ✔ Remove all sources of light from the bedroom (unless you need a soft light to keep the Worry Monster away).

- ✔ Cool down. Body temperature drops to fall asleep (a warm bath or shower actually helps by moving blood circulation closer to skin and away from the body's organs).

- ✔ Eliminate exposure to noise or distractions that could cause waking.

- ✔ If you wake during the night, avoid turning on lights.

- ✔ Practice a ritual for preparing to sleep (for example, read a book, take a hot bath or shower).

What If the Worry Monster Still Won't Go Away?

If you have tried the strategies presented in this book and the Worry Monster is still bullying you and making it hard to enjoy life, it may be time to talk to a professional. Also, if the strategies in this book aren't effective, it may mean that your worry and fear are too big at this point for your plan to work. Sometimes we need to have help and support from an expert, even if our parents are already trying to help us. Some parents have their own struggles with the Worry Monster and don't even realize that they are worrying as much as their kids! Once most parents learn about the Worry Monster and how to keep him in line, they can be good helpers to keep the Worry Monster from taking over. Of course you may have to remind them to use the tools in this book on their own Worry Monster from time to time. Remember, the Worry Monster visits and bullies people of all ages.

If this is the case, I recommend talking to your parents about finding a counselor or therapist whom you feel comfortable with and who has experience helping children overcome anxiety. I also recommend that you ask what approaches the professional uses. Although there are lots of good ways to help kids with troublesome worries, I suggest working with a professional who uses cognitive behavioral strategies as part of his or her approach. The reason for this is that I know it works, and you already know a lot about it!

Sometimes the Worry Monster and his friends are so strong that even after using the strategies in this book and working with a counselor or therapist, the monsters still won't go away. When this happens, some families consider using medication to help fight the Worry Monster. Again, talk to your parents if your worry and fear are not letting up so they can help you figure out what to try next. Even if you decide to try medication, it is still important to continue counseling and working your plan to get rid of the Worry Monster.

Things to Remember

- ✔ The Worry Monster does not want to go away and can be very stubborn and tricky.

- ✔ Small victories are a step in the right direction.

- ✔ Sometimes adding a new tool or strategy results in a victory.

✔ Diet, exercise, and sleep are important for keeping the Worry Monster away.

✔ Counseling can be very helpful when the Worry Monster won't stop bullying.

Things to Do

✔ Try a new strategy or tool to trick the Worry Monster.

✔ Focus on one small step in your plan.

✔ Change the rewards if current ones aren't working.

✔ Exercise daily, and be mindful of what you are eating and drinking.

✔ Get a good night's sleep.

✔ Talk to your parents about finding a professional to help if the Worry Monster won't go away and you continue feel bad.

CHAPTER 12

Conclusion

All life is an experiment. The more experiments you make the better.

~ Ralph Waldo Emerson

Bringing It Home

Dear Dr. Dan,

I've learned a lot about the Worry Monster with you and when he's giving me worries.... I've learned that the Worry Monster thinks of the thing that a good non-worry kid would say, and then he thinks the opposite and says that to you. So he gives you lots of worries. So if you just overpower him by talking about him and doing lots and lots of practice about him, you will [conquer] your Worry Monster [and have] no worries. Then when you have no worries, you can help your friends not worry.... So I think that the Worry Monster is really bad. So if you ever get the Worry Monster, you should punch him out!

~ eight-year-old warrior

Congratulations! You are now an officially certified Worry Monster Warrior. You know how the Worry Monster works. You know how he triggers the fight or flight response in your brain and body and how he tells you things to make you worried and scared. However, you also know that when you change the way you think or when you do a behavior that the Worry Monster tells you not to, your worry and fear lessen, and you become more confident. That's it! It really is that simple. Of course, we all know, and must remember, that it takes a lot of courage to put these ideas into practice.

The message for you to remember is that worry, fear, and anxiety *can* be overcome. Those feelings are not nearly so powerful when we understand that there is a Worry Monster making us feel them, and like the Wizard of Oz, he is only a pathetic bully behind a curtain. Our worrisome and scary thoughts, given to us by the Worry Monster, are responsible for 99.9% of all of our worry and fear. We need to be aware of our thinking and thoughts—how to identify them and change them into healthier thoughts.

When you are feeling nervous, worried, anxious, or scared:

✔ Ask yourself what you are thinking.

✔ Ask yourself if it is true.

✔ Change your thinking so that it is more realistic.

✔ Do the behavior the Worry Monster is scaring you into not doing.

✔ Smile to yourself, and give yourself a high five or a fist bump because you have just earned another victory over the Worry Monster!

Remember to stay in the present and to breathe—deep, long breaths, in and out. Pick behaviors and strategies that will weaken the Worry Monster, little by little, and increase your self-confidence and inner strength. Then (and you know what I am going to say by now) practice those behaviors over and over and over again!

Always remember that the Worry Monster is trying to trick us into not living to our fullest life potential. You are a Warrior

now. You now have the tools to defeat him! Show him who's boss!
Send him away! He is no match for you and your team. Look at
him now. You can't see him? That's because he is running scared.
Reading this book has made him worried and weak. Go get him!
It is time to finish him off! You can do this!

Suggested Reading and Resources

For Children

Crist, J. J. (2004). *What to do when you're scared and worried: A guide for kids*. Minneapolis, MN: Free Spirit.

Henke, K., & Hamilton, L. (2010). *Wemberly worried*. Pine Plains, NY: Live Oak Media.

Lester, H. (2003). *Something might happen*. Boston: Houghton Mifflin/ Walter Lorriane Books.

Maier, I. (2004). *When Lizzy was afraid of trying new things*. Washington, DC: Magination Press.

Viorst, J. (1987). *Alexander and the terrible, horrible, no good, very bad day*. New York: Aladdin.

Willems, M. (2005). *Leonardo, the terrible monster*. New York: Hyperion.

For Adolescents

Adderholdt, M., & Goldberg, J. (1999). *Perfectionism: What's bad about being too good?* Minneapolis, MN: Free Spirit.

Hipp, E. (2008). *Fighting invisible tigers: A stress management guide for teens* (3rd ed.). Minneapolis, MN: Free Spirit.

Rivero, L. (2010). *The smart teens' guide to living with intensity.* Scottsdale, AZ: Great Potential Press.

Tompkins, M. A., & Martinez, K. M. (2013). *My anxious mind: A teen's guide to managing anxiety and panic.* Washington, DC: Magination Press.

For Parents

Barlow, D. H., & Craske, M. G. (2007). *Mastery of your anxiety and panic* (4th ed.). New York: Oxford University Press.

Dalai Lama, & Cutler, H. C. (1998). *The art of happiness: A handbook for living.* New York: Riverwood Books.

Gilman, B. J., Lovecky, D. V., Kearney, K., Peters, D. B., Wasserman, J. D., Silverman, L. K.,…Rimm, S. B. (2013). *Critical issues in the identification of gifted students with co-existing disabilities: The twice-exceptional.* http://sgo.sagepub.com/content/3/3/2158244013505855.full

Greene, R. W. (2014). *The explosive child: A new approach for understanding and parenting easily frustrated, chronically inflexible children* (5th ed.). New York: HarperCollins.

Greenspon, T. S. (2002). *Freeing our families from perfectionism.* Minneapolis, MN: Free Spirit.

Kurcinka, M. S. (2006). *Raising your spirited child: A guide for parents whose child is more intense, sensitive, perceptive, persistent, and energetic* (rev. ed.). New York: HarperCollins.

Levine, M. (2012). *Teach your children well: Parenting for authentic success.* New York: HarperCollins.

Liebgold, H. (2004). *Freedom from fear: Overcoming anxiety, phobias, and panic.* New York: Kensington.

Paterson, R. J. (2000). *The assertiveness workbook: How to express your ideas and stand up for yourself at work and in relationships.* Oakland, CA: New Harbinger.

Reivich, R., & Shatté, A. (2002). *The resilience factor: 7 keys to finding your inner strength and overcoming life's hurdles.* New York: Broadway Books.

Rivero, L. (2010). *A parent's guide to gifted teens: Living with intense and creative adolescents.* Scottsdale, AZ: Great Potential Press.

Seligman, M. E. P. (1996). *The optimistic child: A proven program to safeguard children against depression and build lifelong resilience.* New York: Houghton Mifflin.

Seligman, M. E. P. (1998). *Learned optimism: How to change your mind and your life.* New York: Pocket Books.

Seligman, M. E. P. (2002). *Authentic happiness: Using the new positive psychology to realize your potential for lasting fulfillment.* New York: Free Press.

Webb, J. T., Gore, J. L, Amend, E. R., & DeVries, A. R. (2007). *A parent's guide to gifted children.* Scottsdale, AZ: Great Potential Press.

Zucker, B. (2009). *Anxiety-free kids: An interactive guide for parents and children.* Waco, TX: Prufrock Press.

Additional Resources

Taming the Monster DVD by Dan Peters, Ph.D.: www.summitcenter.us

Shrinking the Worry Monster children's books and parenting seminars by Sally F. Baird, Ph.D., R.N.: www.SallyBairdphd.com

Additional Resources for Promoting Healthy Communities

Challenge Success: www.challengesucess.org

Race to Nowhere: www.racetonowhere.com

Fostering Resilience: www.fosteringresilience.com

Mental Health America: www.mentalhealthamerica.net

Resiliency in Action: www.resiliency.com

Let's Erase the Stigma: www.lets.org

Endnotes

Introduction
1   National Institute of Mental Health, n.d.

Chapter 2
2   Liebgold, 1998b
3   Barlow & Craske, 2007
4   Liebgold, 1998a, 1998b
5   Tompkins & Martinez, 2013

Chapter 3
6   Greenspon, 2002
7   Silverman, 2009
8   Greenspon, 2002
9   Adderholdt & Goldberg, 1999

Chapter 4
10   Liebgold, 1998b

Chapter 5
11   Zucker, 2009
12   Liebgold, 2004
13   Barlow & Craske, 2007

Chapter 6
14   Beck, 1979; Ellis & Harper, 1979
15   Liebgold, 1998b
16   Zucker, 2009

Chapter 7
17   Dalai Lama & Cutler, 1998
18   Dalai Lama & Cutler, 1998, p. 268
19   Barlow & Craske, 2007

Chapter 8

20 Skinner, 1965
21 Liebgold, 2004
22 Liebgold, 1998b
23 Scott, 2013
24 Adderholdt & Goldberg, 1999
25 Reivich & Shatté, 2002

Chapter 10

26 Liebgold, 1998b

Chapter 11

27 Tomkins & Martinez, 2013
28 Liebgold, 2004
29 Liebgold, 2004
30   National Sleep Foundation, n.d.
31 Knop, 2009

References

Adderholdt, M., & Goldberg, J. (1999). *Perfectionism: What's bad about being too good?* Minneapolis, MN: Free Spirit.

Barlow, D. H., & Craske, M. G. (2007). *Mastery of your anxiety and panic* (4th ed.). New York: Oxford University Press.

Beck, A. T. (1979). *Cognitive therapy and the emotional disorders.* New York: Penguin.

Dalai Lama, & Cutler, H. C. (1998). *The art of happiness: A handbook for living.* New York: Riverwood Books.

Ellis, A., & Harper, R. A. (1979). *A guide to rational living* (3rd ed.). North Hollywood, CA: Wilshire Books.

Greenspon, T. S. (2002). *Freeing our families from perfectionism.* Minneapolis, MN: Free Spirit.

Knop, N. (2009). *Sleep to learn: Recent research.* California Association of Independent Schools (CAIS) faculty newsletter. Retrieved from www.caisca.org/page/22434_Archived_Publications.asp

Liebgold, H. (1998a). *Children's curing anxiety, phobias, shyness and obsessive compulsive disorders: The phobease way* (5th ed.). Retrieved from www.angelnet.com

Liebgold, H. (1998b). *Curing anxiety, phobias, shyness and obsessive compulsive disorders: The phobease way* (5th ed.). Retrieved from www.angelnet.com

Liebgold, H. (2004). *Freedom from fear: Overcoming anxiety, phobias, and panic.* New York: Kensington.

National Institute of Mental Health. (n.d.). *What is anxiety disorder?* Retrieved from www.nimh.nih.gov/health/topics/anxiety-disorders/index.shtml#part4

National Sleep Foundation. (n.d.). *Children and sleep/Teens and sleep.* Retrieved from www.sleepfoundation.org/article/sleep-topics/children-and-sleep; www.sleepfoundation.org/article/sleep-topics/teens-and-sleep

Reivich, K., & Shatté, A. (2002). *The resilience factor: 7 keys to finding your inner strength and overcoming life's hurdles.* New York: Broadway Books.

Scott, E. (2013). *The stress management and health benefits of laughter.* Retrieved from http://stress.about.com/od/stresshealth/a/laughter.htm

Silverman, L. K. (2009). Petunias, perfectionism, and level of development. In S. Daniels & M. M. Piechowski (Eds.), *Living with intensity Understanding the sensitivity, excitability, and emotional development of gifted children, adolescents, and adults.* Scottsdale, AZ: Great Potential Press.

Skinner, B. F. (1965). *Science and human behavior.* New York: Free Press.

Tompkins, M. A., & Martinez, K. M. (2013). *My anxious mind: A teen's guide to managing anxiety and panic.* Washington, DC: Magination Press.

Zucker, B. (2009). *Anxiety-free kids: An interactive guide for parents and children.* Waco, TX: Prufrock Press.

Index

About the Author

 Dan Peters, Ph.D., is a licensed psychol-
ogist who has devoted his career to the
assessment and treatment of children,
adolescents, and families, specializing in
those who are gifted, creative, and
twice-exceptional (2e). As a parent of
three children, he understands the daily
challenges of raising children in today's
world, as well as the importance of teaching them coping skills, problem solving,
and resilience. He is passionate about
creating healthy communities by helping parents and teachers
engage children in the classroom, at home, and in life so that they
can realize their full potential.

Dr. Peters is co-founder and Executive Director of the Summit
Center, where he is available for consultation. He serves on the
California Association for the Gifted (CAG) Advisory Board,
the Supporting Emotional Needs of the Gifted (SENG) Editorial
Board, the Advisory Board for the 2e Center for Research and
Professional Development at Bridges Academy, and as Co-Chair of
the Assessments of Giftedness Special Interest Group of the National
Association for Gifted Children (NAGC). He speaks regularly at

state and national conferences on a variety of gifted, learning, and parenting topics, including how to overcome worry and anxiety. Dr. Peters is co-author (with Dr. Susan Daniels) of *Raising Creative Kids* (Great Potential Press, 2013), as well as many articles on topics related to parenting, giftedness, twice-exceptionality, dyslexia, and anxiety. He is also co-founder of Camp Summit, a sleep-over summer camp for gifted youth. He lives in Northern California with his wife and three children.